The Deen Bros.

Get Fired Up

The Deen Bros.

Get Fired Up

GRILLING, TAILGATING, PICNICKING, AND MORE

Jamie and Bobby Deen

and Melissa Clark

BALLANTINE BOOKS ✦ NEW YORK

Copyright © 2011 by Deen Brothers Enterprises, LLC
Photographs copyright © 2011 by Ben Fink Photography

Published in the United States by Ballantine Books, an imprint of
The Random House Publishing Group, a division of Random House, Inc., New York

BALLANTINE and colophon are registered trademarks of Random House, Inc.

Library of Congress Cataloging-in-Publication Data

Deen, Jamie.
    The Deen Bros. get fired up: grilling, tailgating, picnicking, and more / Jamie and
Bobby Deen, and Melissa Clark.
        p. cm.
    Summary: "The Deen Brothers present 100 all-new recipes and entertaining ideas
for outdoor gatherings"—provided by publisher.
    Includes index.
    ISBN 978-0-345-51363-2
    eBook ISBN 978-0-440-42364-5
    1. Outdoor cooking. 2. Cooking, American—Southern style. 3. Cookbooks.
I. Deen, Bobby. II. Clark, Melissa. III. Title.
    TX823.D44 2011
    641.5'78—dc22   2010047462

Printed in the United States of America on acid-free paper

www.ballantinebooks.com

9 8 7 6 5 4 3 2 1

First Edition

Book design by Liz Cosgrove

This is for Aunt Peggy,
and in loving memory of Uncle George.
Because y'all did, we can.

Contents

Introduction

When we were boys, we'd run in through the front door after school, stop in the kitchen to grab a snack, then head right out the back door in about the time it takes to shout, "Mama, we're home!" Mama used to call us a couple of yard apes, we spent so much of our childhood outside. We don't have holes in the knees of our dungarees or scrapes on our elbows anymore, and our lives are a bit more complicated than they used to be, but we still love to fly straight out that back door as often as we can. The only difference is that now, we're not just tossing around a ball back there, we're cooking dinner at the same time.

For a couple guys like us, whose lives—at work and at home—revolve around food, cooking out in the fresh air is pure recreation. It's about the simple joy of being outdoors, taking it easy, and working up a major appetite. Whether we're doing **BBQ chicken** (see page 10) and **Grilled Red Pepper and Bow Tie Pasta Salad** (page 72) for a weeknight supper, or we're gathering around with a bunch of friends for our **Grilled Low Country Boil** (page 181), cooking outside is our ideal way to end any day—even days spent cooking in the kitchen of The Lady & Sons! And over the years, we've grilled, picnicked, tailgated, and beach bummed our way into more than a cookbook's worth of favorite recipes. So we figure it's about time we shared them with y'all.

These aren't recipes for entertaining in grand style. Most of the food in this book is made for paper plates, not good china (well, you might want a nice platter for the **Grilled Lobster Tails with Spicy Butter** [page 182], but you don't need more than one hand to eat half the things in this book). Fancy or not, the foods we're sharing here make for special meals. Eating them is a memorable occasion because it's so fun just being outside.

Everyone loves a backyard barbecue, and we're no different. Just the smell of one of our neighbors out grilling is enough to get us going. You sniff that good smoke in the air and you know they're having fun. Then, before you know it, you're so hungry you've got to figure out a way to get invited, or head out and grill up something for yourself. The best thing about grilling might just be that it's the perfect excuse for kicking back and doing less work, since cooking outside almost always means more hands on deck, less mess, and more time to goof off and enjoy yourself. When else do you invite folks over, tell them to bring the beer, let them do the cooking, then send 'em home saying, "Best party ever, man!"

Some of our tastiest meals are the lazy ones that happen when we're sitting out back with a cold drink on a hot night. "What happens if you bust out a tube of biscuit dough and throw it over the coals?" we might ask. (The answer, on page 53, is some completely awesome biscuit flatbread!) We do tend to get experimental whenever we find ourselves wondering what's for dinner. "Hey," we'll say, "why can't you give a nice big burger the taco-night treatment?" (You can! See **Mexican Fiesta Burgers,** page 96.)

We don't limit our grilling to the backyard either. As you may know, Jamie considers tailgating at a Georgia Bulldogs game to be a sporting event in its own right. From the back of his truck, he'll grill you up everything from **Spicy Prosciutto-Wrapped Shrimp and Scallop Skewers** (page 90) to a **Hot Buffalo Burger with Blue Cheese** (page 103). Then there's the stuff we like to pack up the night before we leave, from our **Game Day Breakfast to Go** (think biscuit, ham, cheese, and eggs; page 115) to some pregame snacks that we bust out while the coals get going. Something about a sporting event seems to speed up everyone's metabolism, so it's never too early for **Creamy Ham and Pickle Roll-Ups** (page 120) or **Chili-Topped Overstuffed Potatoes** (page 118).

Working on this book, we got to revisit all those memories of past summers and favorite recipes. Of course, the weather didn't always cooperate. Since we tested these recipes year-round, we had the opportunity to picnic indoors quite a bit, and we can tell you that while a big blanket on the grass in the warm sun helps set the scene, at the end of the day, it's the food that makes a great picnic. Whether you're packing up some **TGIF Chicken Salad Wraps with Pimiento** (page 139) and a container of **NOLA-Style Dirty Rice Salad** (page 156) for a day at the park or a brown bagger's workday lunch, you're bringing the good times with you wherever you go.

That's the spirit that inspired this book. To us, cooking outside is an opportunity to celebrate living in this beautiful country, our own beloved Southern landscape, and take the time to enjoy great meals with great people. We hope you'll make our recipes part of your backyard barbecues, picnics, tailgating parties, or beach trips, too. Now y'all go on outside and work up an appetite!

On the Grill

Growing up in Albany, Georgia, we were always outside kids. From an early age we were running around barefoot, making a mess of our clothes and being total boys. Considering that we love to be outdoors and we love food and cooking, it's no surprise that we're natural-born grillers.

As with a lot of families, our dad was the one who grilled. He'd be out there lining up barbecued chicken or ribs on a big old cooker that he'd fashioned out of a fifty-gallon oil drum cut in half and welded back together with some hinges and racks (also known as a Texas hibachi), and our mouths would just be watering while we tossed around a football or a baseball. So grilling has always seemed like play to us. You get yourself a cold drink in one hand, a pair of tongs in the other, leave the dirty dishes in the kitchen, and invite over enough friends, and you hardly know you're lifting a finger to make the meal happen. Plus, anytime there's more meat and less mess on the menu is a good time in our book!

Because we are lucky enough to have such great weather here in Savannah, we cook outside as often as we can, even when there's no special occasion. Bobby has been known to make **Balsamic Cherry Pork Chops** (page 18) or **Pesto Chicken Breasts with Sun-Dried Tomatoes and Mozzarella** (page 11) on his little charcoal grill any night of the week, and we both love to fire up the big gas grill if we've got a bunch of folks coming over and we're doing something more ambitious like **Down-Home Baby Back Ribs** (page 23).

In the great gas or charcoal debate, we're nonpartisan. We use both. Gas is convenient and cooks nice and clean, but we grew up with the flavors and smells of charcoal and wood smoke, and sometimes that's just what we want. Plus, we know a lot of grill masters who pride themselves on keeping a coal or wood fire going at just the right temperature; it's definitely an art. For those who'd rather push a button, or who want to know that the heat will stay low and slow for as long as it takes to get even the biggest **Kielbasa-Stuffed Whole Turkey Breast** (page 16) perfectly cooked and golden, gas is nice and reliable.

Whether you're doing a **Big, Fat, Garlicky Rib Eye** (page 32) for two or a **Smoky Pork Butt** (page 26) for ten, grilling is about the least-fussy way to get your meat superflavorful. One of Bobby's favorites to throw on the grill is **Herb-Rubbed Pork**

Tenderloin (page 24) because it's nice and lean. And who wouldn't lust for a simple charred steak like our Cracked Black Pepper Skirt Steak (page 27)?

Truth be told, Bobby inherited our daddy's preference for meat a little this side of well-done (Mama just called it burnt), while Jamie sides with Mama in preferring meat that's more likely to get up and walk off the plate. So the backyard grill is our peacekeeper: We can take a few steaks off first for the rare-meat lovers, then leave some on longer, and we can grill a big hunk of meat till the ends are brown and crispy, and still be sure to have some rosier slices at the center or closer to the bone.

But grilling up a great meal isn't always about hunks of meat. Maybe because we never felt the need to clutter our kitchen with a panini press, we discovered that a grill is actually the best place to cook up a bunch of hot sandwiches all at once. Not only does it add a nice smoky flavor and crispy browned texture, but you can also set up an assembly line and make enough for a party's worth of folks. You'll want to, because everyone loves a hot sandwich stuffed with meat, cheese, and maybe some coleslaw or pickles in there as well, all layered on buttered, grill-toasted bread. Try our Miami Cubano with Ham, Cheese, and Pickles (page 49) and you'll know what we're getting at when we say these grilled sandwiches are like a ray of sunshine breaking through a cloudy day.

Let's not forget that side dishes can taste just as good as the mains when cooked on a hot, smoky grill. From an elegant hors d'oeuvre like Prosciutto-Wrapped Asparagus (page 68) to a familiar dish with a twist like Smoky Potato Salad with Horseradish Mayo (page 66), we love to use our imaginations to put the grill to use with whatever suits the menu and the season best. We always say you can serve the same burgers or chicken over and over—and Beer Can Chicken with Sweet and Spicy Pickled Vidalia Onions (page 13) is certainly one we never tire of—because as long as you mix up the sides, it's a whole new ball game every time.

If you've got a great view from out back, like Bobby does, or an active five-year-old, like Jamie and Brooke do, you're probably outside most of the time already, so why not get cooking? If you've got friends on hand who want to help, hand them an apron; if they don't, hand them a margarita. We'll take both, please!

1
Chicken, Steaks, and Other Hunks of Meat

All-Points Chicken

We have a saying when we are at a loss as to what to make for a family dinner: All roads point to chicken! Thankfully, it is no different on the grill. We came up with four ways to cook our favorite bird—one for every point on the compass.

West: Spicy Cowboy Style, with Smoky Chiles

We often wonder what dinners would have been like if we had achieved our childhood ambitions of growing up to be cowboys. No doubt this firey chicken (maybe with a side of Smoky Potato Salad with Horseradish Mayo, page 66) would be on the menu every night. **Serves 2 to 4**

One 3½-pound whole chicken, rinsed and patted dry

2 tablespoons olive oil

1½ tablespoons chopped chipotle chile in adobo sauce from a can or jar

1 tablespoon finely chopped garlic

2 teaspoons chopped fresh sage or ¼ teaspoon dried sage

Salt and freshly ground black pepper

---

1. To butterfly the chicken, place the chicken on a clean cutting board, breast side facing down. Holding the tail of the chicken, use kitchen shears to cut along each side of the backbone, from end to end. Remove and discard the backbone. Look for a patch of white cartilage at the base of the inner breastbone; make a cut in the cartilage (this will help to release the breastbone). Grasp each side of the chicken and bend the chicken backward until you hear a crack. Pop out the breastbone, which will be exposed beneath.

2. In a small bowl, whisk together the olive oil, chipotle, garlic, and sage.

3. Season the chicken all over with salt and pepper. Brush generously with the chipotle mixture. Cover the chicken with plastic wrap and let marinate at room temperature for 45 minutes.

4. Preheat the grill to high heat and brush the grate with oil or spray with nonstick cooking spray.

5. Transfer the chicken, skin side down, to the grill. Close the cover and cook until the juices run clear when the chicken is pricked in the thigh with a fork and the skin is lightly charred, 12 to 14 minutes per side.

East: Asian-Style Wings, with Soy Sauce and Ginger

Sesame seeds make this chicken festive and fun. We love the combination of sweet and salty that the soy sauce and honey bring to the table. If your family prefers a meatier piece of chicken (a drumstick rather than a wing), you can still use this fantastic marinade: Just add a little more time on the grill—5 to 7 minutes per side for white meat, 10 to 12 minutes per side for dark. **Serves 4**

¼ cup soy sauce	2 tablespoons peanut oil
¼ cup finely chopped scallions (white parts only), chopped greens reserved for garnish	1½ tablespoons sesame oil
3 tablespoons honey	2 pounds chicken wings, rinsed and patted dry
2 tablespoons grated fresh ginger	2 tablespoons sesame seeds, for garnish

1. In a large bowl or shallow baking dish, whisk together the soy sauce, scallions, honey, ginger, peanut oil, and sesame oil. Reserve ¼ cup of the marinade, then place the chicken in the bowl or dish. Cover the chicken with plastic wrap and let marinate at room temperature for 45 minutes.

2. Preheat the grill to medium-high heat and brush the grate with oil or spray with nonstick cooking spray.

3. Remove the wings from the marinade and place on the grill. Close the cover and cook, basting occasionally with the reserved marinade, until the chicken is cooked through and slightly charred, 4 to 5 minutes per side. Sprinkle the chicken with sesame seeds and scallion greens while hot.

GAS VERSUS CHARCOAL

Truth be told, we generally use our gas grill when we're grilling at home. Since it can be preheated and ready to go with just the flick of a switch and a turn of the dial, it's just easier. And we Deens like to take it easy.

On the other hand, charcoal-burning kettle grills are great when you don't have a lot of space to set up the grill or if you want to wheel it over to one section of your yard. Building a fire with the coals is part of the DIY fun of cooking outdoors, and you can buy different varieties of wood chips (such as cherry, alder, or pine) to mix in with the charcoal to enhance the flavor.

Naturally, when we are out tailgating, we use a small, portable hibachi grill. Compact and charcoal fueled, it is the perfect solution for when you're grilling away from home.

North: Deli Style, Stuffed with Corned Beef and Mustard

On our trips up north to New York, we can't get enough corned beef on rye, piled high with sauerkraut, cheese, and plenty of mustard. Consider this our version of that sandwich—with the chicken subbed in for the bread. If you want to take it one step further, serve it with pickle spears on the side. **Serves 4**

2 bone-in split chicken breasts (about 3 pounds), rinsed and patted dry	¼ cup grated **Swiss cheese** (1 ounce)
½ teaspoon salt, plus additional to taste	¼ cup olive oil
½ teaspoon freshly ground black pepper, plus additional to taste	2 tablespoons Dijon mustard
	Dill pickle spears for serving (optional)
3 ounces thinly sliced corned beef	
¼ cup sauerkraut, drained well	4 metal skewers

1. Cut a deep, 3-inch-long pocket horizontally in each chicken breast half. Season the chicken all over with the additional salt and pepper to taste.

2. Fill each pocket with one-fourth each of the corned beef, sauerkraut, and Swiss cheese (some filling will be visible).

3. In a small bowl, whisk together the olive oil, mustard, the ½ teaspoon salt, and the ½ teaspoon pepper. Brush the chicken generously with the mixture. Use a metal skewer to secure each breast closed.

4. Preheat the grill to high heat and brush the grate with oil or spray with nonstick cooking spray.

5. Transfer the chicken to the grill. Close the cover and cook until the chicken is just cooked through and the skin is lightly charred, 7 to 8 minutes per side.

South: What Else but BBQ?

Here in the South, when you tell your friends and family you're fixing to fire up the grill, you're usually talking about one thing—BBQ chicken. Every family has its own special recipe. This is ours, the one we use at home or in the kitchen of The Lady & Sons. Serve it with plenty of Classic Southern Slaw (page 149) and a pitcher of Cucumber Sangría (page 197) and you've got yourself a backyard party to remember.

Serves 2 to 4

One 8-ounce can tomato sauce
⅓ cup apple cider vinegar
3 tablespoons molasses
2 tablespoons dark brown sugar
2 tablespoons ketchup
2 tablespoons minced onion
1 tablespoon grated fresh ginger

2 garlic cloves, finely chopped
1 jalapeño pepper, seeded, if desired, and minced
½ teaspoon salt, plus additional to taste
¼ teaspoon freshly ground black pepper, plus additional to taste
One 3½-pound whole chicken, rinsed, patted dry, and cut into 8 pieces

1. In a medium saucepan over medium heat, combine the tomato sauce, vinegar, molasses, brown sugar, ketchup, onion, ginger, garlic, jalapeño, the ½ teaspoon salt, and the ¼ teaspoon pepper. Simmer the sauce until slightly thickened, about 15 minutes.

2. Season the chicken pieces all over with the additional salt and pepper to taste. Transfer to a large bowl. Pour two-thirds of the barbecue sauce over the chicken (reserve the rest for basting). Cover with plastic wrap and let marinate at room temperature for 45 minutes.

3. Preheat the grill to medium-high heat and brush the grate with oil or spray with nonstick cooking spray.

4. Transfer the chicken pieces to the grill. Close the cover and cook, basting occasionally with the reserved sauce, until the chicken is cooked through and well glazed, 5 to 7 minutes per side for white meat, 10 to 12 minutes per side for dark.

Pesto Chicken Breasts with Sun-Dried Tomatoes and Mozzarella

As Bobby is fond of saying, there's no tastier way to eat heathfully than grilling chicken breasts. Searing it adds so much flavor, then we punch it up here even more with an Italian-inspired combo of pesto sauce, sun-dried tomatoes, and a little bit of mozzarella cheese (to cut some calories, try using low-fat mozzarella). You can buy good prepared pesto in the refrigerated section of the supermarket, or you can make your own fresh at home (see below). That fresh basil taste just can't be beat! **Serves 4**

Four 8-ounce boneless, skinless chicken breasts, rinsed and patted dry
Salt and freshly ground black pepper
⅓ cup chopped sun-dried tomatoes packed in oil
4 ounces mozzarella cheese, grated (about 1 cup)

½ cup prepared pesto sauce (found in the refrigerated section of the supermarket) or Homemade Pesto (see box)

4 metal skewers

---

1. Cut a deep, 3-inch-long pocket horizontally in each chicken breast. Season the chicken inside and out with salt and pepper.

2. Fill each breast with one-quarter each of the tomatoes and mozzarella cheese. Use a metal skewer to secure each breast closed and brush generously with the pesto sauce.

3. Preheat the grill to medium-high and brush the grate with oil or spray with nonstick cooking spray.

4. Place the chicken on the grill. Close the cover and cook, basting occasionally with any remaining pesto, until the chicken is cooked through and lightly charred, 4 to 5 minutes per side.

Homemade Pesto

Makes 1 cup pesto sauce

4 ounces fresh basil, rinsed and trimmed (about 5 cups)
¾ cup extra-virgin olive oil
½ cup pine nuts or slivered almonds
2 garlic cloves, coarsely chopped
½ teaspoon salt

Combine the basil, olive oil, pine nuts, garlic, and salt in the bowl of a food processor or blender; purée until smooth. The sauce can be stored in the refrigerator, covered, for up to 1 week or frozen for up to 6 months.

Beer Can Chicken with Sweet and Spicy Pickled Vidalia Onions

In our family, you bet Beer Can Chicken is a staple. We're always adding new twists to the recipe. Lately we've been hooked on serving it with these fantastic quick-pickled Vidalia onions—a classic Southern ingredient with an addicting amount of kick and pucker. No surprise here, but a Beer Can Shandy (page 197) goes really well with this dish. **Serves 4**

3 tablespoons olive oil	One 3½-pound whole chicken, rinsed and patted dry
2 tablespoons Dijon mustard	Salt and freshly ground black pepper
1 tablespoon light brown sugar	One 14.9-ounce can beer
2 teaspoons chili powder	Sweet and Spicy Pickled Vidalia Onions (see
2 garlic cloves, finely chopped	below), for serving

1. In a small bowl, combine the olive oil, mustard, brown sugar, chili powder, and garlic.

2. Season the chicken generously inside and out with salt and pepper. Slather the chicken inside and out with the mustard mixture.

3. Prepare the grill for indirect grilling (see page 22) and preheat to medium-high heat.

4. Pop open the beer can and pour out (or slurp up) the top 2 inches of beer. Place the beer can on a solid surface away from the grill. Place the bird cavity over the beer can.

5. Stand the chicken and beer upright on the grill grate. Close the cover and cook until the juices run clear when the chicken is pricked in the thigh with a fork, about 1¼ hours.

6. Remove the chicken from the grill and let stand for 10 minutes before carving. Serve with Sweet and Spicy Pickled Vidalia Onions.

Sweet and Spicy Pickled Vidalia Onions

Makes 2 cups pickled onions

1 large Vidalia onion, thinly sliced crosswise
1 tablespoon apple cider vinegar
1 teaspoon kosher salt
Pinch of cayenne pepper
Pinch of sugar

Place the onion in a bowl. Toss with the vinegar, salt, cayenne, and sugar. Let the mixture stand for at least 30 minutes before serving.

Peachy Chicken Legs

There is nothing that signals a Georgia summer's day more than the sweet aroma of peaches, especially when it's mixed with the smoke coming off the grill. Jamie got the idea to add fresh ginger to these chicken legs to make them even better. Delicious! **Serves 4**

2 pounds chicken drumsticks and thighs	**1 tablespoon balsamic vinegar**
Salt and freshly ground black pepper	**1 tablespoon finely chopped fresh ginger**
¼ cup peach jam	**2 teaspoons finely chopped garlic**

1. Place the chicken pieces into a bowl and season generously with salt and pepper.

2. In a small bowl, combine the peach jam, vinegar, ginger, and garlic. Spoon half the jam mixture over the chicken and toss to coat (reserve the rest for basting). Cover the bowl with plastic wrap and let marinate at room temperature for 45 minutes.

3. Preheat the grill to high heat and brush the grate with oil or spray with nonstick cooking spray.

4. Transfer the chicken pieces to the grill. Close the cover and cook, basting occasionally with the reserved peach mixture, until the juices run clear when the chicken is pricked in the thigh with a fork and the skin is well glazed, 10 to 12 minutes per side.

Fresh Ginger Makes It Smooth

We just love cooking with fresh ginger. Most large supermarkets these days carry it, you just need to know where to look (usually near the onions and garlic). So when you see some, go ahead and pick it up. It's terrific in this Peach Chicken Legs recipe, but you can also grate it up and stir it into your favorite marinades and sauces. We also really love to throw it in the blender with yogurt, peaches, and bananas for a fresh-fruit breakfast smoothie. A little honey makes it even better.

Stuffed Turkey Cutlets with Corn and Black Beans

We love to take advantage of turkey cutlets as another healthier option for the grill. This is a great way to serve them that's on the spicier side—just the way we like it. **Serves 4**

2 tablespoons olive oil, plus additional for brushing
½ cup finely chopped onion
¾ cup canned black beans, rinsed and drained
½ cup frozen corn kernels, thawed
2 tablespoons chopped fresh basil
½ teaspoon Tabasco or other hot sauce

½ teaspoon kosher salt, plus additional to taste
4 turkey cutlets (about 1 pound)
Freshly ground black pepper
Sour cream, for serving (optional)
Guacamole, for serving (optional)

4 metal skewers

1. In a medium skillet over medium-high heat, warm the olive oil. Add the onion and cook, stirring, until translucent, about 5 minutes. Add the black beans and corn and cook for 2 minutes more. Stir in the basil, Tabasco, and the ½ teaspoon salt.

2. Season the turkey cutlets on both sides with the additional salt and pepper to taste. Spread the corn filling over the tops of each cutlet, leaving a ½-inch border on all sides to prevent leakage. Roll the cutlets up over the filling and use a skewer to secure closed. Brush the outside of each turkey roll with olive oil.

3. Preheat the grill to medium and brush the grate with oil or spray with nonstick cooking spray.

4. Transfer the turkey rolls to the grill. Close the cover and cook, turning occasionally, until the turkey is just cooked through, 4 to 5 minutes per side.

5. Slice the turkey rolls crosswise and serve with a dollop of sour cream and a dollop of guacamole, if desired.

The Good Times Are in the Details . . .

Another fun thing about grilling is playing with all the toys—we mean the tools—you get to go with it. While some tools and gadgets are unnecessary, you can't grill without long-handled tongs, a long-handled basting brush, metal skewers, a grilling basket, and a good pair of heavy-duty grilling gloves. These simple items will make your outdoor cooking experience much more enjoyable.

Kielbasa-Stuffed Whole Turkey Breast

We have yet to do our Thanksgiving turkey on the grill (and this may be the year!), but this sausage-stuffed turkey breast is a reason to be thankful anytime of the year. Smoky kielbasa flavor makes a great partner to turkey, and the citrusy honey mustard sauce brings it together with a zing. If you're really, really feeling the turkey-day vibe, try serving this with our Grilled Brown Sugar Brussels Sprouts (page 63). Come springtime, it's phenomenal with Prosciutto-Wrapped Asparagus (page 68). **Serves 6**

One 2½-pound boneless turkey breast
Salt and freshly ground black pepper
One 6-ounce link smoked kielbasa
Olive oil, for brushing

¼ cup honey mustard, plus additional for serving (optional)
1 tablespoon freshly squeezed orange juice
1 teaspoon finely grated orange zest

1. Insert a long, flexible knife, such as a boning knife, lengthwise through the center of the turkey breast, cutting one slit, end to end. Wiggle the knife around to make a pocket wide enough to fit the kielbasa.

2. Season the turkey with salt and pepper. Slide the kielbasa into the pocket. Brush the outside of the turkey with the olive oil.

3. In a small bowl, whisk together the honey mustard, orange juice, and orange zest.

4. Preheat the grill to medium heat and brush the grate with oil or spray with nonstick cooking spray.

5. Transfer the turkey to the grill. Close the cover and cook until an instant-read thermometer inserted into the breast reads 145°F, 40 to 45 minutes. Brush generously with the honey mustard mixture. Close the cover and continue to cook, turning occasionally, until the temperature reaches 155°F, about 10 minutes.

6. Let stand for 5 minutes before slicing (the meat will continue to cook to 170°F while resting). Serve with honey mustard on the side, if desired.

Balsamic Cherry Pork Chops

We love to serve "the other white meat" because it's a tremendously satisfying and versatile lean protein that packs a flavor wallop. This balsamic cherry glaze adds a touch of elegance. You'll see that the dish looks like fancy, company-is-coming food, but, believe us, it is so easy to put together you can have it for a weekday grilling treat. This makes a good-looking plate with one of our Grilled Tomatoes with Parmesan and Herbs (page 62) served alongside. **Serves 4**

2 tablespoons plus 2 teaspoons olive oil
¼ cup finely chopped onion
2 garlic cloves, finely chopped
¼ cup balsamic vinegar
3 cups frozen cherries, chopped
¼ cup chicken stock

3 tablespoons cold butter, cut into cubes
½ teaspoon salt, plus additional to taste
½ teaspoon freshly ground black pepper,
  plus additional to taste
Four 5- to 6-ounce bone-in pork chops (¾ inch thick)

1. Heat 2 tablespoons of the olive oil in a large skillet over medium heat. Stir in the onion and garlic and cook, stirring, for 2 minutes. Stir in the vinegar and cook for 30 seconds. Add the cherries and chicken stock and increase the heat to high. Cook until the liquid is thick and slightly syrupy, 5 to 7 minutes. Whisk in the cold butter, the ½ teaspoon salt, and the ½ teaspoon pepper. Transfer half of the cherry glaze to a separate bowl and reserve.

2. Coat the pork chops with the remaining 2 teaspoons oil and season generously with the additional salt and pepper to taste. Brush the chops with half of the cherry glaze.

3. Preheat the grill to high heat and brush the grate with oil or spray with nonstick cooking spray.

4. Transfer the chops to the grill. Close the cover and cook until the meat is cooked through, 4 to 5 minutes per side.

5. Let the chops rest for 5 minutes before serving, with the reserved cherry glaze spooned on top.

Take Five Before Digging In

Letting the meat rest after cooking allows the juices to settle in—instead of seeping out of the cut. The thicker the meat, the longer you should let it rest. Five minutes will do the trick for a pork chop; plan on 30 minutes for a whole shoulder roast.

Spicy Sesame Pork Ribs

This is a recipe we came up with when we wanted to re-create the spareribs we often get on pupu platters in Chinese restaurants. After a little (tasty) trial and error, we discovered the secret ingredient is a splash of sherry. As a bonus, when you make a whole meal out of these bite-size ribs, you don't have to tussle with your brother over who gets more! **Serves 4**

3 pounds pork spareribs, rinsed and patted dry
½ cup hoisin sauce
3 tablespoons sherry
3 tablespoons sesame oil
3 tablespoons finely chopped fresh ginger
1½ tablespoons soy sauce

1 tablespoon rice vinegar
1 large garlic clove, finely chopped
½ teaspoon crushed red pepper flakes
Salt and freshly ground black pepper
1 tablespoon sesame seeds, for garnish

1. Place the ribs in a wide, shallow nonreactive container.

2. In a small bowl, whisk together the hoisin sauce, sherry, sesame oil, ginger, soy sauce, vinegar, garlic, and red pepper flakes. Pour the mixture over the ribs and turn to coat. Cover with plastic wrap and refrigerate for at least 4 hours or overnight.

3. Remove the ribs from the refrigerator. Scrape off any excess marinade from the ribs and reserve. Season the ribs generously with salt and pepper.

4. Prepare the grill for indirect grilling (see page 22), preheat to medium-high heat, and brush the grate with oil or spray with nonstick cooking spray.

5. Place the ribs over indirect heat (the unlit portion of the grill). Close the cover and cook, turning and basting occasionally with the reserved marinade, for 1 hour. Continue cooking until the ribs are fork tender and easily separate from the bone, 30 minutes to 1 hour.

6. Place the ribs on a plate, sprinkle with sesame seeds, and serve.

Cook Slow, Play Fast

When we've got something slow cooking on the grill like ribs, we like to play a little tag football and let the fire work its magic. Losing team is in charge of cleanup!

Direct and Indirect Heat

We talk a lot in this book about grilling with direct and indirect heat. So listen up! This is the part where we explain what that means and how to do it, whether you use a gas or charcoal grill.

Direct Heat This is grilling, plain and simple. Direct heat is for when you need to sear a Cracked Black Pepper Skirt Steak (page 27), quick-cook Pesto Shrimp Skewers (page 88), or seal in the flavor of a nice, juicy Ultimate Onion Burger (page 99). For a gas grill, all you have to do is adjust the heat to the desired temperature (usually medium-high). Let the grill preheat for 5 to 15 minutes (depending on the grill size; check the instructions that came with the grill) and you're ready to go. For a charcoal grill, simply rake the coals into a pile in the center of the grill. Place the food in the center where the heat will be the highest—if necessary, you can push the food to the outside of the grill where the temperature will be lower to finish cooking or if it starts to burn.

Indirect Heat Traditionally, this is the way you grill when you're doing large pieces of meat like pork shoulder or beef brisket or whole chickens or fish. We also use indirect heat to do some things that are not so traditional, like Grilled Pepperoni Pizza (page 54) and Biscuit Flatbreads Three Ways (page 53). The indirect heat lets you cook the thin crust all the way through (even melting the cheese on top) without burning it.

For a gas grill with two burners, turn one burner on and put the food over the other, unlit burner. If the grill has four or more burners, light the burners on the outside of the grill and put the food over the unlit burners in the middle. Some gas grills have an upper rack, away from the heat. This rack can be very handy for toasting bread or melting cheese, because any heat you get up on the rack will be indirect heat.

For a charcoal grill, rake the coals to both sides of the grill, leaving an open space in the middle. This way the heat will surround the food (indirectly) without getting too hot underneath it. Or, if you have a smaller charcoal grill, you can just rake the coals to one side and put the food on the side without the coals.

The most important thing about indirect heat is to keep the grill lid closed while the food is grilling. Opening it up to check (or steal a taste!) will release some of the heat and the food will take even longer to cook.

Down-Home Baby Back Ribs

The secret to the classic, down-home flavor of these ribs is the low, indirect heat and the slow cooking—you just can't rush a rack of ribs or the ribs will dry out. Grillers everywhere have a long tradition of debating the merits of the sauce versus the rub for their ribs. We like to be diplomatic and use both. Trust us, we make this favorite over and over again for our family and friends because we know that this is what they want! **Serves 4 to 6**

2 tablespoons kosher salt
2 tablespoons dark brown sugar
1 tablespoon sweet paprika
2 teaspoons garlic powder
2 teaspoons dry mustard powder
1½ teaspoons freshly ground black pepper
1 teaspoon onion powder

1 teaspoon hot paprika
1 teaspoon dried oregano
½ teaspoon celery seed
2 racks baby back pork ribs (4 to 5 pounds)
½ cup freshly squeezed orange juice
¼ cup apple cider vinegar

1. To make the rub, mix the salt, brown sugar, sweet paprika, garlic powder, mustard powder, pepper, onion powder, hot paprika, oregano, and celery seed in a bowl, breaking up any lumps in the brown sugar or garlic powder with your fingers.

2. To prepare the ribs, place the ribs, meat side down, on a rimmed baking sheet. Slide your fingers under the thin membrane in the middle of the rack and peel it off. Repeat with the second rack.

3. Transfer 1 tablespoon of the rub to a small bowl for serving and divide the remaining rub between the 2 racks of ribs, rubbing it into the meat.

4. Prepare the grill for indirect grilling, preheat to medium heat, and brush with oil or spray with nonstick cooking spray. Alternatively, preheat the oven to 325°F. If using the grill, place a large roasting pan beneath the unlit portion of a gas grill or on the portion of a charcoal grill without briquettes.

5. When ready to cook, place the ribs, bone side down, on the grate over the roasting pan and away from the direct heat. Close the cover and cook for 20 minutes. Alternatively, place the ribs on a rimmed baking sheet and bake for 20 minutes.

6. Meanwhile, in a small bowl, whisk together the orange juice and vinegar. After the ribs have cooked for 20 minutes, brush them with the orange juice mixture. Close the cover and continue to grill over indirect heat or bake until the meat is fork tender, an additional 1 hour and 40 minutes, brushing it with sauce every 20 minutes.

7. If using the oven, light the broiler and broil the ribs under direct heat for 3 minutes per side. If using the grill, shift the ribs over to direct heat and grill, uncovered, for 3 minutes per side.

8. Let the ribs rest for 5 to 10 minutes before cutting them for serving. Sprinkle with the reserved rub before serving.

Herb-Rubbed Pork Tenderloin

This takes a little bit of time but not a lot of effort to prepare. Let the tenderloin sit in the marinade overnight and you will be rewarded with the juiciest, most succulent piece of meat imaginable. And the crisp herb-laden crust that forms on the meat after grilling makes this dish a showstopper. It tastes absolutely fantastic with a side of Balsamic-Glazed Portabellos with Goat Cheese (page 74).   **Serves 4 to 6**

2 large garlic cloves, finely chopped	**2 tablespoons finely chopped fresh rosemary**
2 teaspoons salt	**2 tablespoons chopped fresh thyme**
¼ cup olive oil	**2½ teaspoons freshly ground black pepper**
1½ tablespoons red wine vinegar	**Two 1-pound pork tenderloins**
2 tablespoons chopped fresh sage	

1. Using a mortar and pestle or the flat side of a knife, mash the garlic with 1 teaspoon of the salt until it forms a paste. Transfer the garlic paste to a small bowl. Whisk in the olive oil, vinegar, sage, rosemary, thyme, pepper, and the remaining 1 teaspoon salt.

2. Smear the mixture all over the pork. Transfer the pork to a bowl. Cover tightly with plastic wrap and refrigerate for at least 1 hour or overnight. Let come to room temperature before grilling.

3. Preheat the grill to medium-high heat and brush the grate with oil or spray with nonstick cooking spray.

4. Transfer the pork to the grill. Close the cover and cook, turning once, until a dark golden crust forms on the pork and the meat is just cooked through, 7 to 9 minutes per side.

5. Let the pork rest on a cutting board for 5 minutes before slicing and serving.

Got a Big Piece of Meat? Grill It Fail-Safe and Fearless

If you want to be sure a big piece of meat like a pork tenderloin is perfectly cooked through and nice and juicy—and you don't much care about the char—try this fail-safe method. Wrap the meat in aluminum foil and prick the foil all over to let the heat in and some of the steam out. Then grill as usual. This way, you can get a little of that smoky taste, all the convenience and easy cleanup of grilling, but less of the superdark, unpredictable char that can make grilling a larger cut tricky.

Smoky Pork Butt

This is our tried-and-true family recipe, seasoned just the way Mama taught us. Folks, you don't mess with a winner! Pork butt (also sold as pork shoulder or pork blade shoulder) tends to be a fattier cut of the pig and makes for some unbelievably tender and juicy roasts. Be sure to save yourself some leftovers for pulled pork sandwiches (see page 46) with plenty of Classic Southern Slaw (page 149). **Serves 8 to 10**

For the spice rub

1½ tablespoons **The Lady's House Seasoning** (see below)

1 tablespoon light brown sugar

1 tablespoon dry mustard powder

½ teaspoon celery seed

One 7- to 8-pound bone-in pork shoulder

For the barbecue sauce

3 cups apple cider vinegar

1¼ cups ketchup

⅔ cup packed light brown sugar

⅓ cup **Dijon mustard**

2 tablespoons Worcestershire sauce

1 tablespoon chili powder

2 teaspoons salt

1. To make the spice rub, in a small bowl, combine the Lady's House Seasoning, brown sugar, mustard powder, and celery seed. Rub the mixture all over the pork shoulder. Place the pork in a large container and cover tightly with plastic wrap. Refrigerate for at least 1 hour or overnight. Let come to room temperature before grilling.

2. To make the barbecue sauce, combine the vinegar, ketchup, brown sugar, mustard, Worcestershire, chili powder, and salt in a medium saucepan over medium heat. Simmer until slightly thickened, 15 to 20 minutes. Pour half the sauce over the pork (reserve the rest for basting).

3. Prepare the grill for indirect grilling, preheat to medium-low heat, and brush the grate with oil or spray with nonstick cooking spray. Place a roasting pan beneath the unlit portion of a gas grill or on the portion of a charcoal grill without briquettes to catch any fat drippings.

4. Place the pork on the grate over the roasting pan. Close the cover and cook, basting every 30 minutes with the reserved sauce, until the meat is fork tender and the bone separates easily from the meat, 5 to 6 hours.

5. Let the pork stand on a cutting board for 30 minutes. Slice and serve with any remaining sauce or use for pulled pork sandwiches.

The Lady's House Seasoning

Makes 1½ cups seasoning

1 cup salt
¼ cup freshly ground black pepper
¼ cup garlic powder

In a small bowl, combine the salt, pepper, and garlic powder. Transfer to an airtight container and store at room temperature for up to 6 months.

Cracked Black Pepper Skirt Steak

This is a fantastic preparation that makes this affordable cut of meat tender and gives it so much flavor. We often serve this thinly sliced on a bed of mixed greens; the meaty, garlicky juices double as an out-of-this-world salad dressing. **Serves 4**

2 garlic cloves, finely chopped	1 tablespoon cracked black pepper
1 teaspoon kosher salt, plus additional to taste	¼ teaspoon dried oregano
1½ pounds skirt steak	2 teaspoons olive oil

1. Using a mortar and pestle or the flat side of a chef's knife, mash the garlic with the 1 teaspoon salt until it forms a paste.

2. Rub the steak all over with the garlic paste. Season the steak lightly with the additional salt, the pepper, and oregano. Coat the steak with the olive oil.

3. Preheat the grill to high and brush the grate with oil or spray with nonstick cooking spray.

4. Transfer the steaks to the grill. Close the cover and cook to desired doneness, 2 to 3 minutes per side for medium-rare.

5. Let the steaks rest for 5 minutes on a platter or cutting board before slicing thinly and serving.

MAINTAINING YOUR OUTDOOR GRILL

Every grill is a little different, so be sure you read (and follow) the manufacturer's instructions. That said, every grill grate will benefit from a quick scrub with a good, sturdy grill brush both before and after cooking. Brushing your grill grate with oil or spraying with nonstick cooking spray will keep it free of rust when you're not using it and prevent food from sticking to the grate when you are. A gas grill may have small holes under the grate or in the lid (these are called "deflectors"). Make sure you go over them with a stiff wire brush once in a while so they don't get clogged with ash or soot, as this will interfere with temperature control.

Five-Star Filet Mignon Stuffed with Mushrooms and Onions

Normally it's a rib eye that we throw on the grill, but for those nights when we want something a little extra special, nothing less than filet mignon will do. We love it stuffed with mushrooms and sweet Vidalias, and served with even more mushrooms on top. If you didn't know better, you'd think it came out of a five-star restaurant rather than your own backyard. **Serves 6**

4 tablespoons (½ stick) unsalted butter
1 Vidalia onion, finely chopped
1 tablespoon finely chopped fresh rosemary
4 cups diced portabello mushrooms (about 2 large mushrooms)
½ cup dry white wine
¼ teaspoon salt, plus additional to taste

¼ teaspoon freshly ground black pepper, plus additional to taste
Six 8-ounce filet mignon steaks (about 2 inches thick)
Olive oil, for brushing

Grill basket

1. Melt the butter over medium-high heat in a large skillet. Stir in the onion and rosemary. Cook until the onion is slightly translucent, about 2 minutes. Stir in the mushrooms and cook, stirring, until the mushrooms are soft and most of the juices have evaporated, 4 to 5 minutes. Pour in the wine and let simmer until most of the liquid has evaporated, about 2 minutes. Season with ¼ teaspoon each salt and pepper.

2. Cut a deep pocket horizontally into each steak. Season the steaks with the additional salt and pepper to taste. Stuff each pocket with about 1½ tablespoons of the mushroom mixture, reserving the remaining mushroom mixture for serving. Brush the steaks with olive oil.

3. Preheat the grill to medium-high heat.

4. Place the steaks in a grill basket (this way any filling that falls out during cooking won't fall into the fire). Transfer the basket to the grill. Close the cover and cook to desired doneness, 5 to 6 minutes per side for medium-rare.

5. Let the steaks rest for 5 minutes on a platter or cutting board before serving with the remaining mushroom mixture alongside.

How to Tell When Meat Is Done

In general, we don't like to grill with a meat thermometer. Instead, we like to use the hand test to judge when it's time to take the steaks off the grill. It goes like this:

• **For rare:** Press your index finger to the tip of your thumb. With the index finger of your other hand, feel the area of your palm at the base of your thumb—that is what the steak will feel like when it is rare.

• **For medium-rare:** Press your middle finger to the tip of your thumb. With the index finger of your other hand, feel the area of your palm at the base of your thumb—that is what the steak will feel like when it is medium-rare.

• **For medium:** Press your ring finger to the tip of your thumb. With the index finger of your other hand, feel the area of your palm at the base of your thumb—that is what the steak will feel like when it is medium.

• **For well-done:** Press your pinky finger to the tip of your thumb. With the index finger of your other hand, feel the area of your palm at the base of your thumb—that is what the steak will feel like when it is well-done.

Internal-Temperature Guidelines

While we don't bother with meat thermometers when testing steaks, it's wise to use them for larger cuts of meat and poultry. See below for food-safe temps to determine doneness.

• **Ground beef:** 150°F for medium, 170°F for well-done

• **Beefsteak:** 135°F for medium-rare, 145°F for medium, 155°F for medium-well, 170°F for well-done

• **Pork chops:** 145°F for medium, 170°F for well-done

• **Pork butt:** 170°F for well-done, 180°F for falling-off-the-bone tender

• **Lamb chops:** 135°F for medium-rare, 145°F for medium, 155°F for medium-well, 170°F for well-done

• **Poultry:** 165°F for cooked through

Grilled and Glazed Porterhouse Steak for Two

We like to think of this as the meat lover's version of putting two straws in the same milk shake on date night. It's just plain romantic to share a steak with your sweetie. This said, if we're doing this on a brothers' grilling night, we might just throw one on for each of us with a couple of skewers of Party Chokes (page 89) on the side. **Serves 2**

One 2-pound porterhouse steak (2 inches thick)	**3 tablespoons unsalted butter, melted**
Salt and freshly ground black pepper	**1½ tablespoons Worcestershire sauce**

1. Preheat the grill to medium-high heat and brush the grate with oil or spray with nonstick cooking spray.

2. Season the steak generously with salt and pepper. In a small bowl, whisk the butter and Worcestershire to combine.

3. Transfer the steak to the grill. Close the cover and grill, turning every 2 minutes and brushing with the butter mixture, until cooked to desired doneness, about 15 minutes for medium-rare.

4. Let the steak rest for 5 minutes before slicing and serving.

Big, Fat, Garlicky Rib Eye

When we say we're hungry for steak, a thick-cut, fully marbled rib eye is exactly what we're talking about. It's our favorite cut of meat; at 1½ inches thick, it even makes the butcher jealous! And it's the perfect texture combination, chewy without being tough, and so flavorful it doesn't need much in the way of dressing up. The aroma of the grilling meat alone is just tantalizing; it brings out our inner cavemen—and look out, even salad-loving Bobby has been known to gnaw on the bone! **Serves 2**

2 garlic cloves, minced
1 teaspoon salt

¼ teaspoon freshly ground black pepper
One 17- to 20-ounce rib-eye steak (1½ inches thick)

1. Using a mortar and pestle or the flat part of a chef's knife, smash together the garlic with the salt and pepper until a thick paste forms. Rub the paste all over the steak.

2. Preheat the grill to high heat and brush the grate with oil or spray with nonstick cooking spray.

3. Transfer the steak to the grill. Close the cover and cook to the desired doneness, about 4 minutes per side for rare.

4. Let the steak rest for 5 minutes before slicing and serving.

Mix and Mingle, Y'all!

When we have a big outdoor bash, we like to set up the tables in separate areas of the yard. That way, guests are encouraged to mingle, and there's a big space in the middle cleared for games. (Jack loves hide-and-seek, Jamie and Bobby go for Wiffle ball, and Brooke and Paula throw the Frisbee!)

Dijon New York Strip Steak

This is Jamie's wife Brooke's favorite steak, and it's easy to see why. You'll just love the way the tangy mustard and brown sugar mingle with the beefy juices, so satisfying when served with crusty bread (or our Pizza Flatbreads with Rosemary and Garlic Oil, page 52) to mop up every bit of flavor. And the fact that this is a dinner that goes from zero to ready in less than fifteen minutes counts for another huge plus in the win column. **Serves 2**

Two 8-ounce New York strip steaks (1¼ inches thick)
1 garlic clove, halved
½ teaspoon salt

½ teaspoon freshly ground black pepper
2 tablespoons Dijon mustard
2 teaspoons dark brown sugar

1. Rub the steaks all over with the cut sides of the garlic and season with the salt and pepper. In a small bowl, mix together the mustard and brown sugar and slather the mixture all over the steaks.

2. Preheat the grill to high heat and brush the grate with oil or spray with nonstick cooking spray.

3. Transfer the steaks to the grill. Close the cover and cook to the desired doneness, about 3 minutes per side for medium-rare.

4. Let the steaks rest for 5 minutes before slicing and serving.

Be Prepared for Weeknight Grilling

We think there's no better way to relax after a tough day at work than having a delicious family dinner out on the grill. Weekly schedules being what they are (a race against the clock, basically), you gotta put in a few extra minutes on a Saturday to make sure the grill is ready to go when you want to fire it up later in the week. So use the weekend to give it a good scrub, and check that you've got enough propane or charcoal and that your grill toys—we mean tools—are right where they're supposed to be and haven't migrated to other parts of the house or garage. Then, whenever the weather is fine, you are set to get grillin'!

Burger Pepper Boats with Olives and Scallions

This is something Mama's been making for us since we were little kids no bigger than Jack. She added the chopped olives because of Bobby (he's always been an olive fan), and we still make 'em that way. You should, too, whether or not Bobby is coming over for dinner. **Serves 4**

1½ **pounds ground beef**

6 **tablespoons chopped pimiento-stuffed olives**

⅓ **cup chopped scallions (white and light green parts)**

2 **tablespoons mayonnaise**

2 **teaspoons Worcestershire sauce**

1½ **teaspoons salt**

1½ **teaspoons freshly ground black pepper**

Large pinch of dried oregano

2 **large red or green bell peppers, halved lengthwise, cored, and seeded**

Olive oil, for brushing

---

1. In a large bowl, combine the ground beef, olives, scallions, mayonnaise, Worcestershire, salt, black pepper, and oregano. Pack the bell pepper halves with the meat mixture. Brush the sides and bottoms of the peppers and the top of the filling generously with olive oil.

2. Preheat the grill to high and brush the grate with oil or spray with nonstick cooking spray.

3. Transfer the stuffed peppers, stuffing side down, to the grill. Close the cover and cook until the meat is well browned on top, about 5 minutes. Flip the peppers and continue to grill until the peppers are tender and the meat is cooked through, 5 to 6 minutes more.

Our Favorite Fajitas with Smoky Grilled Guacamole

This is a real family-pleaser. Sometimes the only way we can get Jamie's son, Jack, to eat his steak is to hide it in the guacamole. If you're cooking for the younger set, however, it's best to leave out the jalapeño peppers. If it's just the big kids, go ahead and turn up the heat. **Serves 4 to 6**

For the smoky guacamole	For the steak fajitas
2 ripe avocados, halved, peeled, and pitted	**1½ pounds flank steak**
2 jalapeño peppers	**4 garlic cloves, finely chopped**
Olive oil, for brushing	**1 teaspoon salt, plus additional to taste**
3 tablespoons chopped fresh cilantro	**¼ cup olive oil, plus additional for brushing**
2 tablespoons freshly squeezed lime juice	**1 tablespoon freshly squeezed lime juice**
¾ teaspoon salt	**1½ teaspoons ground cumin**
	¾ teaspoon freshly ground black pepper, plus additional to taste
	½ teaspoon dried oregano
	1 medium green bell pepper, seeded and cut lengthwise into ¼-inch strips
	1 Vidalia onion, cut into ¼-inch-thick slices
	Six 8-inch flour tortillas
	Chopped fresh cilantro, for garnish (optional)
	Grill basket

1. To make the guacamole, preheat the grill to medium-high heat and brush the grate with oil or spray with nonstick cooking spray.

2. Lightly brush the avocados and jalapeños with olive oil. Place both on the grill. Close the cover and cook the avocados until lightly charred, about 1 minute per side. Cook the jalapeños until blistered and softened, 1½ to 2 minutes per side. Remove from the heat and let cool.

3. Once the jalapeños are cool enough to handle, peel and seed them, if slightly less heat is desired. Finely chop the jalapeños, then transfer to a medium bowl and combine with the avocados, cilantro, lime juice, and salt. Mash to the desired consistency. Cover the bowl tightly with plastic wrap and refrigerate until ready to use.

4. To make the fajitas, place the steak in a shallow nonreactive bowl. Using a mortar and pestle or the flat side of a chef's knife, mash together the garlic and the 1 teaspoon salt to form a paste. Whisk in the olive oil, lime juice, cumin, the ¾ teaspoon black pepper, and the oregano. Pour the marinade over the steak. Turn to coat. Cover the bowl with plastic wrap and refrigerate for at least 1 hour or overnight. Let come to room temperature for 30 minutes before grilling.

(continued on page 38)

5. Preheat the grill to medium-high heat and brush the grate with oil or spray with nonstick cooking spray.

6. Brush the bell peppers and onions with olive oil and season with the additional salt and pepper to taste. Place the onions in a single layer in a grill basket. Transfer the basket to the grill. Close the cover and cook until the onions are soft and slightly charred, 4 to 5 minutes per side. Transfer the onions to a plate.

7. Arrange the bell peppers in a single layer in the grill basket. Transfer the basket to the grill. Close the cover and cook until the bell peppers are tender and slightly charred, 2 to 3 minutes per side. Transfer the bell peppers to a plate.

8. Increase the heat to high. Remove the steak from the marinade. Transfer the meat to the grill. Close the cover and cook to the desired doneness, 4 minutes per side for medium-rare. Let the meat rest for 5 minutes on a cutting board before slicing into thin slices.

9. Place the tortillas on the grill and cook, uncovered, until lightly colored, about 1 minute per side. Fill the tortillas with steak slices, bell peppers, and onions. Top with the guacamole. Roll up the tortillas and serve, garnished with cilantro if desired.

The Family That Plays Together . . .

Remember, folks, football is not the only sport (really, we checked). Set up backyard games like croquet, horseshoes, or lawn darts—games the whole family can play together.

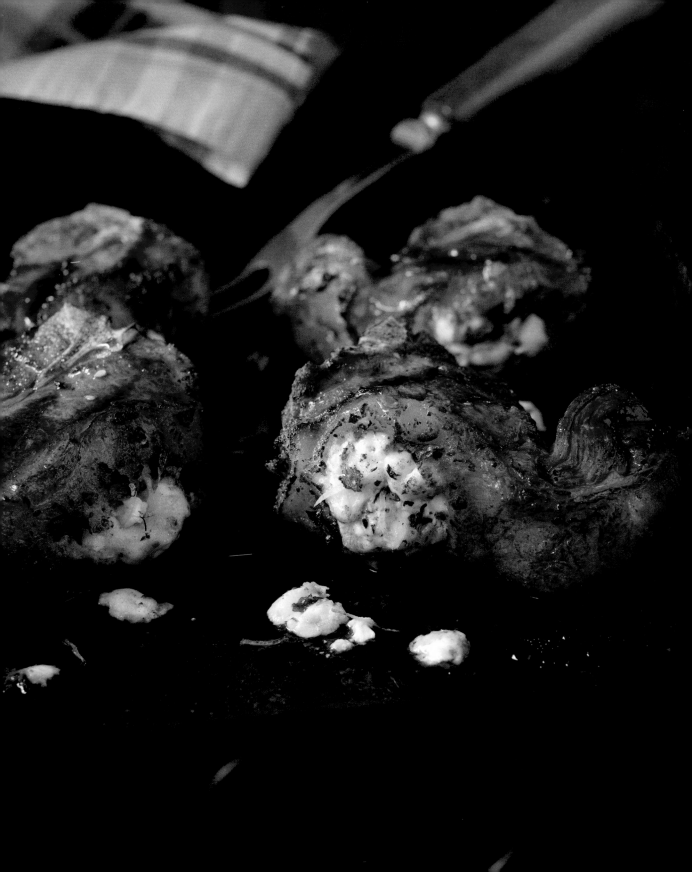

Minty Lamb Chops Stuffed with Feta and Lemon

Mint and lamb are another classic combination, and here the lemon and feta keep it fresh tasting and make it a standout—and it's one of Brooke's favorites, so we just had to share it with everybody. With its Mediterranean-accented flavor, it goes great with Charred Zucchini and Eggplant with Basil Green Goddess Dressing (page 67). **Serves 4**

Four 6-ounce loin lamb chops (1½ inches thick)	**1 tablespoon finely chopped fresh mint**
2 garlic cloves	**1 teaspoon finely grated lemon zest**
Salt and freshly ground black pepper	**Olive oil, for brushing**
½ cup crumbled feta cheese (2 ounces)	

1. Cut a deep pocket horizontally into the chops. Cut 1 garlic clove in half. Rub the cut sides of the garlic halves all over the chops, especially on and around the bone. Season the chops all over with salt and pepper.

2. Finely chop the remaining garlic clove. In a small bowl, combine the feta, mint, chopped garlic, and lemon zest. Stuff the pockets of the lamb with the feta mixture. Brush the chops with olive oil.

3. Preheat the grill to medium-high and brush the grate with oil or spray with nonstick cooking spray.

4. Transfer the lamb chops to the grill. Close the cover and cook to the desired doneness, 3 to 4 minutes per side for medium-rare.

5. Let the chops rest on a platter or cutting board for 5 minutes before serving.

A Little Something Sweet · GRILLED BUTTERY POUND CAKE

Buttery pound cake gets a little caramel-y char when placed on the grill. With a topping of cold whipped cream and fresh fruit, this is a griller's dessert delight. **Serves 4**

One 12-ounce pound cake
5 tablespoons unsalted butter, melted
¼ cup packed light brown sugar

1. Cut the pound cake into ¾-inch-thick slices.

2. In a small bowl, whisk together the butter and brown sugar. Brush both sides of the cake slices with the butter mixture.

3. Preheat a grill to medium-high and brush the grate with oil or spray with nonstick cooking spray.

4. Place the cake slices on the grill. Close the cover and cook until the cake slices are caramelized and golden, about 1 minute per side.

5. Top with fresh berries or peaches and whipped cream to serve.

2

Hot Sammies, Flatbreads, and Pizzas

Classic Pulled Pork Sammies

This recipe is meant to use the leftovers from the Smoky Pork Butt, but to be perfectly honest, we are open to grilling a pork butt just to make these fantastic sammies. If the South produced no other signature dish, these gloriously messy sandwiches would be enough to put the region on the culinary map. **Serves 4**

2½ cups shredded **Smoky Pork Butt (page 26)**
1½ cups prepared barbecue sauce or homemade
   (see page 10)

4 kaiser rolls, split
Classic Southern Slaw (page 149) or bread-and-
   butter pickles, for serving (optional)

In a large bowl, stir together the shredded pork and barbecue sauce. Sandwich the pork mixture, slaw, and pickles (if using) between the split rolls and serve.

Heat It Up Before You Eat It Up

If you are using leftover Smoky Pork Butt for this recipe, you'll want to heat it up before mixing it with the barbecue sauce. If you're doing this out on the grill, place the meat in a large aluminum pan, drizzle it with water to make sure the pork stays moist (beer works great for this, too, if you happen to have it handy), and cover the pan with foil. Place it over indirect heat and let it warm up for 30 minutes. If you're doing this sammie indoors, just set the pan in a 225°F oven. Or you can put the meat in a microwave-safe dish and stick it in the microwave for a minute or so. Any which way, give the meat a good stir before adding the sauce.

Miami Cubano with Ham, Cheese, and Pickles

Now, this is not a sandwich that we grew up on; but we sure have come to love it, and it's become one of our grilling go-tos. Seriously—ham and roast pork and Swiss cheese? Covered with pickles? What is not to love? And finishing it off on a smoky grill makes it taste even better. Serve it with Grilled Red Pepper and Bow-Tie Pasta Salad (page 72) to round out your meal. **Serves 4**

Four 8-inch hoagie rolls, split	**½ pound thinly sliced deli ham**
Melted butter, for brushing	**½ pound thinly sliced roast pork**
2 tablespoons Dijon mustard	**Thinly sliced dill pickles, for topping**
1 pound thinly sliced Swiss cheese	

1. Preheat the grill to medium-high heat and brush the grate with oil or spray with nonstick cooking spray.

2. Brush the inside of each roll with butter. Place each roll, cut sides down, on the grill. Toast the rolls, uncovered, until lightly colored, about 30 seconds.

3. Spread the rolls with mustard. Divide half the Swiss cheese among the 4 rolls. Top with the ham, pork, pickles, and the remaining Swiss cheese. Press the sandwiches together to close.

4. Transfer the sandwiches to the grill. Close the cover and toast for 1 minute per side. Move the sandwiches to the upper rack, or away from the direct heat, of the grill. Close the cover and continue to cook until the filling is hot and the cheese is melted, about 5 minutes.

Zesty Grilled Veggie Sandwich

You will be amazed at how grilled veggies just burst with flavor. There's no need for too much in the way of seasoning; fresh garlic and lemon dressing are enough to allow the veggies to shine. This sandwich makes for a hearty lunch that won't weigh you down. **Serves 4**

6 tablespoons unsalted butter, softened

½ cup grated Parmesan cheese (2 ounces)

3 tablespoons freshly squeezed lemon juice

2 large garlic cloves, finely chopped

1½ teaspoons salt

¾ cup olive oil

⅓ cup chopped fresh basil

2 medium zucchini (about 1½ pounds), cut lengthwise into ¼-inch-thick slices

1 large eggplant (about 1 pound), cut lengthwise into ¼-inch-thick slices

1 Vidalia onion, cut into ¼-inch-thick rounds

Four 8-inch hoagie rolls, split

2 large tomatoes (about 1 pound each), thinly sliced

Grill basket

1. In a small bowl, mash together the butter and Parmesan cheese.

2. In a separate bowl, whisk together the lemon juice, garlic, and salt. Whisk in the olive oil and basil. Keeping the vegetables separate from one another, brush both sides of the zucchini, eggplant, and onion slices with the lemon oil.

3. Preheat the grill to medium-high heat and brush the grate with oil or spray with nonstick cooking spray.

4. Place the onion slices in a single layer in a grill basket. Transfer the basket to the grill. Close the cover and cook until the onions are soft and slightly charred, 4 to 5 minutes per side. Remove the onions to a plate.

5. Place the eggplant and zucchini in a single layer in the grill basket (do this in batches, if necessary). Transfer the basket to the grill. Close the cover and cook until the vegetables are soft and charred around the edges, 3 to 4 minutes per side. Transfer the vegetables to the plate with the onions.

6. Place each roll, cut side down, on the grill. Toast the rolls, uncovered, until lightly colored, about 1 minute.

7. Spread the rolls with the Parmesan butter. Fill the sandwiches with the grilled onions, eggplant, and zucchini and the tomatoes. Press the sandwiches together to close and transfer to the grill. Close the cover and cook until the bread is toasted and the cheese is melted, 1 to 2 minutes per side.

Grilled Philly Cheesesteak

Now, we know cube steak isn't traditionally used for Philly cheesesteak, but we like how tender it is, not to mention quick to prepare. If you want the real deal, substitute a thinly sliced beefsteak, such as beef bottom round or beef eye round. **Serves 4**

1 Vidalia onion, cut into ⅛-inch-thick slices	1 pound cube steak (about ⅛ inch thick)
2½ tablespoons olive oil	Four 8-inch hoagie rolls, split
Salt and freshly ground black pepper	½ pound thinly sliced provolone cheese
1 green bell pepper, seeded and cut into ½-inch-thick strips	Grill basket

1. Preheat the grill to medium-high heat and brush the grate with oil or spray with nonstick cooking spray.

2. Toss the onion slices with 1 tablespoon of the olive oil and season with salt and black pepper. Place in a single layer in a grill basket. Transfer the basket to the grill. Close the cover and cook until the onions are soft and slightly charred, 4 to 5 minutes per side. Transfer the onions to a plate.

3. Toss the bell peppers with 1½ teaspoons of the olive oil and season with salt and black pepper. Arrange in a single layer in the grill basket. Transfer the basket to the grill. Close the cover and cook until the bell peppers are tender and slightly charred, 3 to 4 minutes per side. Transfer the bell peppers to the plate with the onions.

4. Brush the cube steak with the remaining 1 tablespoon olive oil and season with salt and black pepper. Transfer the steak to the grill. Close the cover and cook to the desired doneness, about 1 minute per side for medium-rare. Let stand on a plate for 5 minutes before slicing into ¼-inch-thick strips.

5. Place each roll, cut side down, on the grill. Toast, uncovered, until lightly colored, about 1 minute. Line each roll with about one-quarter of the provolone cheese. Divide the steak, bell peppers, and onions equally among the rolls. Press the sandwiches together to close.

6. Place the sandwiches on the grill. Close the cover and cook, turning once, until the bread is golden and the cheese is melted, about 1 minute per side.

Pizza Flatbreads with Rosemary and Garlic Oil

This makes a nice, thin focaccia-style bread. It's a great side dish or snack, especially when we're serving Pesto Chicken Breasts with Sun-Dried Tomatoes and Mozzarella (page 11) or Italian Chicken and Tricolor Peppers Skewers (page 84), and we find it disappears just as soon as we can pull it off the grill. People do seem to come to our backyard hungry, and this flatbread aims to please! **Makes one 12-inch flatbread**

¼ cup olive oil	½ pound prepared pizza dough
2 teaspoons finely chopped fresh rosemary	Coarse sea salt
1 large garlic clove, finely chopped	

1. In a small bowl, whisk together the olive oil, rosemary, and garlic.

2. On a lightly floured surface, roll the dough into a rectangle about 12 by 7 inches.

3. Preheat the grill to medium-high heat and brush the grate with oil or spray with nonstick cooking spray.

4. Brush the top of the dough with some of the rosemary oil. Transfer the dough, oil side down, to the grill. Close the cover and cook until the bottom is uniformly golden, 2 to 3 minutes. Brush the top of the dough with additional rosemary oil and, using tongs or a heatproof spatula, flip the dough. Close the cover and cook until the bottom is golden, 2 to 3 minutes more (check occasionally to see that it doesn't burn).

5. Brush the top of the bread with additional rosemary oil and sprinkle with sea salt.

Biscuit Flatbreads Three Ways

In the South we just can't have a meal without working some buttermilk biscuits in there somehow. And when we want to do the whole meal outside on the grill, we have to get a little creative; these crispy biscuit flatbreads are the result. Whether topped with ham and Swiss, family-favorite pimiento cheese, or slightly fancier port wine cheese, these biscuit flatbreads are easy and fun to make and so tasty that they might just become the whole reason you fire up the grill. **Serves 8**

One 16.3-ounce can jumbo refrigerated buttermilk biscuits (8 biscuits) ¼ **pound thinly sliced deli ham, cut into ½-inch strips**	¼ **pound thinly sliced Swiss cheese, cut into ½-inch strips**

1. On a lightly floured surface, roll each biscuit into a circle about 4 inches in diameter.

2. Preheat the grill to medium-high heat and brush the grate with oil or spray with nonstick cooking spray.

3. Place the biscuits on the grill. Close the cover and cook until the bottoms are golden, 1 to 2 minutes. Using tongs or a heatproof spatula, flip the biscuits and top with ham and Swiss cheese. Transfer the biscuits to the upper rack of the grill or off the direct heat. Close the cover and cook until the bottoms are golden and the cheese is melted, 2 to 3 minutes.

Note: To make a pimiento cheese or port wine cheese variation, prepare as directed, substituting ½ cup pimiento cheese or port wine cheese spread for the ham and cheese mixture.

Grilled Pepperoni Pizza

Instead of doing another night of take-out from your local pizza place, take it outside and try grilling a crisp-crust, smoke-charred pepperoni pizza in your own backyard. Most supermarkets sell prepared pizza dough in their refrigerated sections. Using it makes this pizza very simple to prepare. You'll never have to tip the delivery guy again. **Serves 4**

1 pound prepared pizza dough, divided into 4 equal-size balls
1 cup tomato sauce

3 cups grated mozzarella cheese (¾ pound)
2 ounces thinly sliced pepperoni

1. On a lightly floured surface, roll each ball of dough into a circle about 7 inches in diameter.

2. Preheat the grill to medium-high heat and brush the grate with oil or spray with nonstick cooking spray.

3. Transfer the dough rounds to the grill. Close the cover and cook until the bottoms are light golden, 1 to 2 minutes. Using tongs or a heatproof spatula, flip and quickly spoon the tomato sauce onto each pizza. Scatter the mozzarella cheese and pepperoni over the pizzas. Close the cover and cook until the bottoms are light golden, about 1 minute.

4. Transfer the pizzas to the upper rack of the grill or off the direct heat. Reduce the heat to medium, close the cover, and cook until the cheese has melted, 3 to 5 minutes.

Grilled Four-Cheese Pizza

This is a grilled pizza for those with more refined tastes. The idea of a white (no tomato sauce) pie might take some getting used to, but once you try this fabulous blend of cheeses, you'll be sold. All you garlic lovers (like Jamie!) will be big fans. And, if you find that you miss the familiar flavor of tomatoes, go ahead and serve up the pizza with our Charred Tomato Salad with Peppers and Onions (page 65). **Serves 4**

¼ cup olive oil
1 garlic clove, thinly sliced
1 pound prepared pizza dough, divided into 4 equal-size balls
1 cup ricotta cheese

One 8-ounce package mozzarella cheese, grated (about 2 cups)
1 cup grated Gruyère or Swiss cheese (4 ounces)
1 cup grated Parmesan cheese (4 ounces)

1. In a small bowl, whisk together the olive oil and garlic.

2. On a lightly floured surface, roll out each dough ball into a circle about 7 inches in diameter.

3. Preheat the grill to medium-high heat and brush the grate with oil or spray with nonstick cooking spray.

4. Brush the tops of the dough rounds with the garlic oil. Transfer, oil side down, to the grill. Close the cover and cook until the bottoms are light golden, 1 to 2 minutes. Brush the tops of the dough rounds with additional garlic oil and flip using tongs or a heatproof spatula. Quickly spread the ricotta cheese over the pizzas and top with the grated mozzarella, Gruyère, and Parmesan cheeses. Close the cover and cook until the bottoms are light golden, about 1 minute.

5. Transfer the pizzas to the upper rack of the grill or off the direct heat. Reduce the heat to medium, close the cover, and cook until the cheeses have melted, 3 to 5 minutes.

Color Me Hungry!

Use brown craft paper instead of a tablecloth for outdoor dining. It makes cleanup much easier, and you can put out a jar of crayons for the kids to color with while they're waiting for second helpings.

On the Grill   Hot Sammies, Flatbreads, and Pizzas

Mini Pizzas on the Grill

As every parent knows, the best way to get your kids to clean their plates is to have them make their own food. For these pizzas, set out their favorite toppings, like sliced pepperoni, chopped black olives, and grated Parmesan, and have the kids pile on as much as they want. Mom and Dad put the pizzas on the grill, and everybody's happy, which is what dinnertime is all about. **Makes 10 mini pizzas**

---

1 pound prepared pizza dough, divided into 10 equal-size balls

10 tablespoons tomato sauce

One 8-ounce package mozzarella cheese, grated (about 2 cups)

---

1. On a lightly floured surface, roll out each ball of dough into a circle about 3 inches in diameter.

2. Preheat the grill to medium-high heat and brush the grate with oil or spray with nonstick cooking spray.

3. Transfer the dough rounds to the grill. Close the cover and cook until the bottoms are light golden, 1 to 2 minutes. Using tongs or a heatproof spatula, flip and quickly spoon 1 tablespoon tomato sauce onto each pizza. Scatter the mozzarella cheese over the pizzas. Close the cover and cook until the bottoms are light golden, about 1 minute.

4. Transfer the pizzas to the upper rack of the grill or off the direct heat. Reduce the heat to medium, close the cover, and cook until the cheese has melted, 3 to 5 minutes.

A Little Something Sweet GINGER-BUTTER GRILLED PEACHES

Here in Georgia we take our peaches very seriously—these peaches with fragrant ginger-butter sauce are seriously good, y'all. **Serves 4**

4 tablespoons (½ stick) unsalted butter
2 tablespoons light brown sugar
1 teaspoon freshly squeezed lemon juice
1 teaspoon pure vanilla extract
¼ teaspoon ground ginger
Pinch of salt
4 ripe peaches, halved lengthwise and pitted

1. In a small saucepan, melt together the butter, brown sugar, lemon juice, vanilla, ginger, and salt.

2. Preheat the grill to high heat and brush the grate with oil or spray with nonstick cooking spray.

3. Brush the peaches with the butter mixture and place on the grill, cut side down. Close the cover and cook, brushing with the butter mixture once halfway through, until the fruit is tender, 2 to 3 minutes per side.

3

Smoky Sides

Mexican Corn on the Cob with Mayo, Lime, and Grated Cheese

We have a rule in our house: You can't grill in the summertime without corn on the cob. It's always on our table, and our Mexican-style version is a big hit. Parmesan, mayo, and a sprinkle of chili powder make it a spicy side dish that is always a winner with grilled meats and fish. It makes a perfect partner to anything from Southern BBQ chicken (see page 10) to Our Favorite Fajitas with Smoky Grilled Guacamole (page 36) to a Zesty Grilled Veggie Sandwich (page 50) and beyond. **Serves 4**

4 ears husked corn on the cob	**Chili powder, to taste**
½ cup mayonnaise	**2 limes, cut into wedges, for serving**
½ cup finely grated Parmesan cheese (2 ounces)	

1. Preheat the grill to medium-high heat and brush the grate with oil or spray with nonstick cooking spray.

2. Slather each ear of corn with 2 tablespoons mayonnaise. Transfer the corn to the grill. Close the cover and cook, turning occasionally, until the corn is lightly charred, 8 to 10 minutes.

3. Immediately coat the corn with the Parmesan cheese and sprinkle lightly with chili powder. Serve with lime wedges.

On the Grill Smoky Sides

Light Up the Night

Christmas in July? Not exactly, but Christmas lights on the patio are a perfect way to light up an after-dark barbecue. Hurricane lanterns work nicely if you don't have access to electrical outlets, and citronella candles will do double duty, lighting up the backyard and keeping mosquitoes at bay.

Grilled Tomatoes with Parmesan and Herbs

Grilled tomatoes are surprisingly easy and look so pretty on the plate. This is a wonderful way to use those early-in-the-season tomatoes. They'll be as ripe and juicy as their August counterparts after a few minutes on the grill. This is one of those side dishes we bust out when we're grilling to impress (in other words, when we're cooking for our mama, Paula). **Serves 4**

2 medium tomatoes (about 1 pound total)	½ cup grated **Parmesan cheese (2 ounces)**
1½ tablespoons olive oil	1 teaspoon dried thyme
½ teaspoon salt	½ teaspoon dried oregano
½ teaspoon freshly ground black pepper	

1. Cut each tomato in half crosswise and, using your fingers or a spoon, gently scoop out the seeds. Place the tomato halves in a medium bowl and toss to coat with the olive oil, salt, and pepper.

2. In a small bowl, stir together the Parmesan cheese, thyme, and oregano. Spoon the cheese mixture over the tomato halves.

3. Preheat the grill to medium-high and brush the grate with oil or spray with nonstick cooking spray.

4. Transfer the tomatoes to the grill, topped side up. Close the cover and cook until the cheese is melted and the tomato skins are slightly blistered, 4 to 5 minutes.

Don't Fear the Winter

One of the reasons off-season grilling is so much fun is that it's unexpected. An investment in an outdoor space heater (or two) will pay for itself with priceless memories of family grilling in the month of December.

Grilled Brown Sugar Brussels Sprouts

Living in Savannah, we are lucky enough to be able to get outdoors and grill all year-round. We like to do Brussels sprouts in the cooler months when corn on the cob is not so readily available. And with their sweetly charred flavor and mouthwatering crunch, grilled sprouts are an unusual Thanksgiving dish that will make you happy all winter long. Try this with our Kielbasa-Stuffed Whole Turkey Breast (page 16). **Serves 6**

3 tablespoons unsalted butter
1½ tablespoons light brown sugar
¼ teaspoon freshly squeezed lemon juice
¼ teaspoon salt
¼ teaspoon freshly ground black pepper

1 pound Brussels sprouts, trimmed and halved lengthwise
Lemon wedges, for serving

Grill basket

1. Preheat the grill to medium-high heat.

2. In a small saucepan over medium-high heat, melt the butter and brown sugar together. Whisk in the lemon juice, salt, and pepper.

3. Toss the Brussels sprouts with the butter mixture in a medium bowl. Arrange the sprouts in a single layer in a grill basket. Transfer the basket to the grill. Close the cover and cook, turning once, until the sprouts are tender and lightly charred, about 3 minutes per side. Serve warm, with lemon wedges.

Charred Tomato Salad with Peppers and Onions

Want to get Jamie to eat his salad? You gotta put it over the fire first. We're willing to bet these charred and toasty-tasting veggies will tempt the salad avoider in your family, too—especially when you serve it along-side a Big, Fat, Garlicky Rib Eye (page 32). **Serves 4**

---

1 medium red bell pepper, seeded and cut lengthwise into quarters

1 medium green bell pepper, seeded and cut lengthwise into quarters

1 Vidalia onion, cut into ¼-inch-thick rounds

1 pint cherry tomatoes

1 tablespoon olive oil, plus additional for brushing

Salt and freshly ground black pepper

2 cups arugula, stemmed, if necessary, and torn into bite-size pieces

1 tablespoon drained capers (optional)

2 teaspoons red wine vinegar

4 metal skewers

Grill basket

---

1. Brush the bell peppers, onions, and tomatoes with olive oil and season with salt and pepper. Thread the tomatoes onto the skewers. Place the onions in a single layer in a grill basket.

2. Preheat the grill to medium-high heat and brush with oil or spray with nonstick cooking spray.

3. Transfer the basket to the grill. Close the cover and cook until the onions are soft and slightly charred, 4 to 5 minutes per side. Transfer the onions to a plate to let cool.

4. Arrange the bell peppers in a single layer in the grill basket. Transfer the basket to the grill. Close the cover and cook until the bell peppers are tender and slightly charred, 2 to 3 minutes per side. Transfer the peppers to the plate with the onions to cool.

5. Place the tomato skewers on the grill. Close the cover and cook, turning occasionally, until the tomatoes are slightly blistered, 2 to 4 minutes total. Let cool.

6. Coarsely chop the onions and bell peppers and combine with the tomatoes in a large bowl. Add the arugula, capers (if using), the 1 tablespoon olive oil, the vinegar, and salt and pepper. Toss well and serve.

Smoky Potato Salad with Horseradish Mayo

In our family we have done potato salad every which way you can think of. We love to serve this quick-and-easy version when we've got the grill fired up. It has the added benefit of letting you prepare it outside, where all the fun is. Credit goes to Uncle Bubba for coming up with the idea to add a little horseradish to give this smoky salad an unexpected kick. **Serves 4**

1½ pounds small- to medium-size Yukon
    Gold potatoes
Olive oil, for brushing
½ teaspoon salt, plus additional to taste
½ teaspoon freshly ground black pepper,
    plus additional to taste

⅓ cup mayonnaise
¼ cup chopped scallions (white and light green
    parts)
3 tablespoons very finely chopped celery
3 tablespoons chopped fresh parsley
2 tablespoons prepared horseradish

1. Prick the potatoes all over with a fork and place on a microwave-safe plate. Cook in the microwave on medium-high power for 3 minutes. Turn the potatoes and cook for 3 minutes more, until fork tender.

2. Preheat the grill to high heat and brush the grate with oil or spray with nonstick cooking spray.

3. Brush the potatoes with olive oil and sprinkle with the additional salt and pepper to taste. Transfer the potatoes to the grill. Close the cover and cook, turning occasionally, until the skins are crisp and dark golden, 7 to 8 minutes. Let the potatoes cool completely, then cut them into large chunks.

4. In a large bowl, combine the potatoes, mayonnaise, scallions, celery, parsley, horseradish, and the ½ teaspoon each salt and pepper. Toss well. Taste and adjust the seasonings, if necessary.

Charred Zucchini and Eggplant with Basil Green Goddess Dressing

We love eggplant and zucchini and would eat them right off the grill, but we try to restrain ourselves because we know they taste so much better with this creamy basil dressing. As an added bonus, if you have any leftover dressing, it'll keep, covered, in the fridge for a few days. It makes a fantastic dip for just about anything: raw veggies, potato chips, anything you've got. **Serves 4**

For the dressing

½ cup sour cream
½ cup packed fresh basil leaves
1 tablespoon freshly squeezed lemon juice, plus additional to taste
1 tablespoon chopped scallion
1 small garlic clove, finely chopped
½ teaspoon salt

For the vegetables

1 large eggplant (1 pound), trimmed and cut crosswise into ¼-inch-thick rounds
2 small zucchini (½ pound), trimmed and cut lengthwise into ¼-inch-thick slices
½ cup olive oil
Salt and freshly ground black pepper

Grill basket

1. To make the dressing, combine the sour cream, basil, lemon juice, scallion, garlic, and salt in a food processor or blender; purée until smooth. Transfer to a small bowl, cover with plastic wrap, and refrigerate until ready to use.

2. To prepare the vegetables, in a large bowl, toss the eggplant and zucchini with the olive oil and season generously with salt and pepper.

3. Preheat the grill to medium-high heat.

4. Arrange the eggplant and zucchini in a single layer in a grill basket (prepare in batches if they don't all fit). Transfer the basket to the grill. Close the cover and cook until the vegetables are tender and charred, 3 to 4 minutes per side.

5. Transfer the eggplant and zucchini to a platter, spoon the basil dressing over, and serve warm or at room temperature.

Prosciutto-Wrapped Asparagus

How do you get your kids to eat asparagus? Wrapping the vegetable in ham doesn't hurt! Now, this is a side dish we could eat eight days a week. But don't skip mixing the lemon zest into the mayo. You will be amazed how much tastier the mayonnaise is—and how much faster those asparagus disappear. We like to make these as a side to Grilled Pepperoni Pizza (page 54) or Grilled Four-Cheese Pizza (page 55). **Serves 4 to 6**

½ cup mayonnaise
1 teaspoon finely grated lemon zest
¾ teaspoon freshly ground black pepper

¾ pound asparagus, ends trimmed
6 ounces thinly sliced prosciutto, torn into
1-inch-wide strips

1. In a long, shallow bowl, whisk together the mayonnaise, lemon zest, and pepper. Dip each asparagus stalk into the mixture and turn to coat evenly. Wrap the length of each asparagus with a strip of prosciutto.

2. Preheat the grill to high heat and brush the grate with oil or spray with nonstick cooking spray.

3. Transfer the asparagus to the grill. Close the cover and cook until the ham is slightly crisp and the asparagus is tender, 1 to 2 minutes per side.

Sweet Potato Coins with Creamy Honey Drizzle

How's this for a side dish that's as pretty as it is practical? Wrapping these buttery sweet potatoes in aluminum foil makes for easy cleanup later. Cutting them up into slices will make them cook a little faster and look good on the plate. And the taste? Absolutely scrumptious. This dish is a win-win-win. **Serves 4**

4 small sweet potatoes (about 2 pounds)	1½ tablespoons honey
8 tablespoons (1 stick) unsalted butter, cut into cubes	¼ cup sour cream
Salt and freshly ground black pepper	¼ cup walnuts, chopped
	1½ tablespoons finely chopped fresh chives

1. Cut the potatoes crosswise into ¼-inch-thick slices. Keeping the coins together in the shape of a potato, transfer each potato to a sheet of aluminum foil. Dot the potatoes with butter cubes and season with salt and pepper. Wrap the foil tightly around the potatoes.

2. Preheat the grill to medium-high heat.

3. Place the potato packets on the grill. Close the cover and cook until the potatoes are fork tender, 15 to 20 minutes.

4. Place the potatoes on serving plates and pull back the foil. Drizzle the potatoes with the honey and top each with a dollop of sour cream. Sprinkle with walnuts and chives and serve.

Grilled Red Pepper and Bow-Tie Pasta Salad

Bow-tie pasta salad is another Southern staple we would never dream of leaving off our family table. We grill the red bell peppers for that great smoky flavor and toss in some peas for the color. The leftovers make a welcome midnight snack, too! This goes with anything, but it's especially great with grilled sammies like the Miami Cubano with Ham, Cheese, and Pickles (page 49) or our Classic Pulled Pork Sammies (page 46).

Serves 4 to 6

1 red bell pepper, seeded and cut lengthwise into quarters
2 teaspoons olive oil
Salt and freshly ground black pepper
6 tablespoons mayonnaise
2 tablespoons finely chopped fresh chives
1 tablespoon balsamic vinegar

4 cups cooked bow-tie pasta (4 ounces dry pasta)
¾ cup frozen peas, thawed
1 cup grated cheddar cheese (4 ounces)
½ cup pitted kalamata olives, sliced

Grill basket

1. In a small bowl, toss the bell peppers with the olive oil and season with salt and pepper.

2. Preheat the grill to medium-high heat.

3. Arrange the bell peppers in a grill basket. Transfer the basket to the grill. Close the cover and cook until the bell peppers are tender and slightly charred, 2 to 3 minutes per side. Cool completely, then cut into ¼-inch-thick strips.

4. In a small bowl, whisk together the mayonnaise, chives, vinegar, and salt and pepper to taste.

5. In a large bowl, combine the pasta, peas, cheddar cheese, bell peppers, and olives. Add the mayonnaise dressing and toss well to coat. Taste and adjust the seasonings, if necessary, before serving.

Balsamic-Glazed Portabellos with Goat Cheese

This dish is in the Smoky Sides chapter, but it would make a great main course if you have any vegetarians at your cookout. Portabello mushrooms have a hearty texture and flavor that is enhanced even further with this balsamic glaze and creamy crumbled goat cheese. If you close your eyes, you might think you've got a mouthful of steak. **Serves 4**

4 portabello mushrooms (about ¾ pound), stems removed	**½ teaspoon freshly ground black pepper**
¼ cup olive oil	**3 ounces goat cheese, crumbled (about ¾ cup)**
3 tablespoons balsamic vinegar	**1½ tablespoons chopped fresh parsley**
½ teaspoon salt	**Grill basket**

1. In a medium bowl, gently toss the mushrooms with the olive oil, vinegar, salt, and pepper.

2. Preheat the grill to medium-high heat.

3. Place the mushrooms in a grill basket. Transfer the basket to the grill. Close the cover and cook until the mushrooms are tender and lightly charred, 2 to 3 minutes per side.

4. Use tongs to arrange the hot mushrooms, stem side up, on a serving plate. Sprinkle with the crumbled goat cheese and the parsley and serve.

A Little Something Sweet GRILLED FIGS, SOUTHERN-STYLE

Here in the South, a lot of folks are lucky enough to have fig trees growing right in their backyards, and we love to grill them up just as fast as we can pick 'em. Grilled figs with butter and brown sugar are fantastic on their own, but you know, they are even better when served with a scoop of butter pecan ice cream. **Serves 4**

4 tablespoons butter, softened
2 tablespoons light brown sugar
8 large figs, cut in half lengthwise
Ice cream for serving (optional)

1. Preheat the grill to medium.

2. In a small bowl, mash up the butter with the brown sugar and roll the mixture into 8 marble-size balls.

3. Press the butter-sugar balls into the cut center of each fig half. Grill the figs, butter side up, until the fig is slightly soft and the butter is melted, 3 to 4 minutes. Serve the figs fresh off the grill on a plate or napkin, or on top of a bowl of your favorite ice cream.

On the Field

When we attend a sporting event—a University of Georgia football game, let's say—we like to get hyped up with team spirit and competitive thrill. So we tailgate. In fact, we've been tailgating in the same spot over at Sanford Stadium for the past five years. Cooking in the shadow of the stadium is a sport in its own right. You may not be at daily team practices, but you've been planning your menu all week long. You're up early the day of the event, you've prepped and packed the night before, and you're keyed up with anticipation of the game and the food. Everything is more fun before a big game, and it's important to put on a spread that matches that level of spine-tingling excitement brought on by a Dawgs-Gators grudge match.

Something about tailgating will turn even a health-minded guy like Bobby into a competitive eater. Tailgating culture is friendly and spirited, with everyone holding a beer and folks you weren't expecting stopping by, so we like to cook up some impressive eats. We want people coming back to cheer at the next game because they remembered the awesome **Spicy Prosciutto-Wrapped Shrimp and Scallop Skewers** (page 90) and **Bacon-and-Cheddar-Stuffed Burgers** (page 97) we made.

Of course, we learned to make a meal in a parking lot from the master: our mama, Paula Deen. Whenever we went to Six Flags or on some trip as a family, Mama would provision our car to be sure we wouldn't need to stop at a restaurant—it was cheaper, and the food was always great. Mama would pick up a roast chicken and turn it into the best sandwich you ever had. To this day we avoid eating at fast food places on the road and instead pack the car to the gills with good eats, thanks to those good memories. We take a page from Mama's approach to on-the-go eating and make ham, egg, and cheese biscuits (we call them **Game Day Breakfast to Go,** page 115), a tradition that gets us out the door bright and early. Mama doesn't tailgate, but she's sure got game!

Jamie is what you'd call a more-than-serious tailgater. In fact, he has a condo right by the Bulldogs stadium in Athens, where he can get all kinds of cooking done in advance, so he can really go overboard. Some games, he'll bring platters of everything from pregame bites like **Chili-Topped Overstuffed Potatoes** (page 118) to **Portabello Pesto Burgers** (page 98), all ready to throw on a grill as soon as he finds a parking space.

Our **Meat 'n' Potato Skewers** (page 83) could make a meal on their own, but we rarely stop there. For good looks, **Italian Chicken and Tricolor Peppers Skewers** (page 84) or **Grilled Ham, Veggie, and Mozzarella Skewers** (page 92) catch people's eyes. We always use 8- to 12-inch-long metal skewers (you'll never have to worry about them burning) and bag up different varieties of prepared skewers separately. Then, once we're at the game, we arrange them all out on the grill together for a great-looking spread. This is just fun food, folks, whether or not your favorite team is playing.

The basic tailgater's trifecta is burgers, dogs, and brews. And we like to spin that classic as many different ways as there are games in the season. You can wake things up with salsa-spiked **Mexican Fiesta Burgers** (page 96) or **Hot Buffalo Burgers with Blue Cheese** (page 103), just to add on to what Jamie calls the best flavor in the world: the flavor of ground beef cooked on a grill outside.

Over the years, we've put about everything we could think of on a burger. And in it. We even took inspiration from our favorite sushi roll for **Spicy Asian Tuna Burgers** (page 104). Bobby, who swears by lean ground turkey, hit on a winner with his **Turkey Burgers with Hummus** (page 105), proving that we do occasionally introduce something a little healthier to the tailgating scene. That's where our **Good Doggies** (hot dogs split and stuffed with lite herb cream cheese and wrapped in turkey bacon; page 108) come in, though, of course, we have our **Bad Doggies** (hot dogs split and stuffed with chipotle cheese, then wrapped in bacon; page 110) days, too. And boy, are those Bad Doggies good!

Even a casual tailgater can cook like a champ with recipes like our awesome glazed **Red Dawgs** (page 107). All you need is a kettle-style grill or some of those portable disposable foil grills you get at a home and garden store. A small grill is ideal for cooking skewers like our **Hawaiian-Style Pork Skewers** (page 87). Thread your skewers the night before, load your cooler in the morning, and before you know it, you're handing out a tasty meal that leaves one hand free for a beer. In this sport, anyone can go pro.

4 Tasty Skewers

Beef Teriyaki Skewers

If you're taking this to tailgate, just zip the threaded skewers in a heavy-duty, resealable plastic bag or store in a plastic container with the marinade and put it in the cooler. By the time you get to the parking lot, the meat will be seasoned to perfection and all set to grill. We like to serve Layered Mandarin Orange Salad (page 152) alongside these skewers. **Serves 6**

1 pound beef bottom round or boneless sirloin, cut into 1½-inch chunks
Salt and freshly ground black pepper
6 tablespoons teriyaki sauce
2 medium green bell peppers, seeded and cut into 1½-inch chunks

1½ tablespoons olive oil, plus additional for brushing
Lemon wedges, for serving

6 metal skewers

Make Ahead

1. In a large bowl, season the beef with salt and pepper. Stir in the teriyaki sauce and cover with plastic wrap. Let stand at room temperature for 30 minutes or refrigerate up to overnight.

2. In a separate bowl, toss the bell peppers with the olive oil and season with salt and pepper.

3. Thread 3 to 5 chunks each of beef and bell peppers onto the skewers, alternating between the two. Pack the skewers in tightly sealed plastic containers to transport in the cooler.

At the Game

1. Preheat the grill to medium-high heat and brush the grate with oil or spray with nonstick cooking spray.

2. Transfer the skewers to the grill. Close the cover and cook, turning once halfway through, until the bell peppers are tender and the beef is cooked to the desired doneness, 1 to 2 minutes per side for medium-rare. Serve with lemon wedges.

Meat 'n' Potato Skewers

Sometimes all you want is a no-frills dish of steak and potatoes to fortify yourself for the big game. These skewers are our easy-to-eat tailgater's version. They sure do hit the spot! **Serves 6**

½ cup steak sauce
1 teaspoon Tabasco or other hot sauce
1 pound beef bottom round or boneless sirloin, cut into 1½-inch chunks
Salt and freshly ground black pepper

1 pound small red creamer potatoes
1½ tablespoons olive oil

6 metal skewers

Make Ahead

1. In a large bowl, stir together the steak sauce and Tabasco. Season the beef with salt and pepper. Add the beef to the bowl and toss well to coat with the steak sauce mixture. Cover the bowl with plastic wrap and let stand at room temperature for 30 minutes or refrigerate up to overnight.

2. Place the potatoes in a microwaveable container and cook in a microwave on high heat until almost tender, about 5 minutes. Toss the potatoes with the olive oil and season with salt and pepper.

3. Thread the beef and potatoes onto the skewers. Pack the skewers in tightly sealed plastic containers to transport in the cooler.

At the Game

1. Preheat the grill to medium-high heat and brush the grate with oil or spray with nonstick cooking spray.

2. Transfer the skewers to the grill. Close the cover and cook, turning once, until the potatoes are tender and the beef is cooked to the desired doneness, about 2 minutes per side for medium-rare.

Tailgating—It's in the Bag

Bring plenty of heavy-duty garbage bags for post-tailgating cleanup; you'll definitely need them. And don't forget the clear recycling bags, too. It's much easier to recycle cans and bottles as you go rather than trying to separate them out when you get home after a long day at the stadium.

Italian Chicken and Tricolor Peppers Skewers

Chicken and veggies make for a great skewer when you want something a little on the lighter side. We brush these with plenty of balsamic vinaigrette to keep the chicken moist and give a nice tanginess to the peppers. These skewers are a snap to put together and make a colorful addition to any party. **Serves 6**

1 pound boneless, skinless chicken breasts, cut into 1½-inch chunks

Salt and freshly ground black pepper

¼ cup homemade balsamic vinaigrette (see below) or bottled balsamic vinaigrette

1 red bell pepper, seeded and cut into 1½-inch chunks

1 green bell pepper, seeded and cut into 1½-inch chunks

1 yellow bell pepper, seeded and cut into 1½-inch chunks

6 metal skewers

Make Ahead

1. Season the chicken with salt and pepper. Place the chicken in a bowl with 2 tablespoons of the balsamic vinaigrette and toss well to combine. Cover the bowl with plastic wrap and let stand at room temperature for 30 minutes or refrigerate up to overnight.

2. In a separate bowl, toss the bell peppers with the remaining 2 tablespoons vinaigrette.

3. Thread 3 to 5 chunks of bell peppers and chicken onto the skewers, alternating between the two. Pack the skewers in tightly sealed plastic containers to transport in the cooler.

At the Game

1. Preheat the grill to medium-high heat and brush the grate with oil or spray with nonstick cooking spray.

2. Transfer the skewers to the grill. Close the cover and cook, turning once halfway through, until the peppers are charred and tender and the chicken is just cooked through, 3 to 5 minutes per side.

Balsamic Vinaigrette

Makes a generous ½ cup vinaigrette

2 tablespoons balsamic vinegar
½ teaspoon salt
Freshly ground black pepper
½ cup extra-virgin olive oil

In a small bowl, whisk together the vinegar, salt, and pepper to taste. Slowly whisk in the olive oil. Store in an airtight container at room temperature for up to 4 hours or in the refrigerator for up to 1 week.

Hawaiian-Style Pork Skewers

When you tailgate as much as we do, you've got to keep upping the ante on your skewers. If the guy next to you starts to grill pork, you grill pork and pineapple. If somebody else dips skewers in peanut sauce, you dip in peanut sauce and honey-roasted peanuts. Believe us, the parking lot is every bit as competitive as the game! You can find jarred peanut sauce in the international or Asian food section of your supermarket.
Serves 6

Two 1¼- to 1½-pound boneless pork tenderloins, cut into 1½-inch chunks	6 cups pineapple chunks
Salt and freshly ground black pepper	2 tablespoons olive oil, plus additional for brushing
½ cup prepared peanut sauce, plus additional for serving	Chopped honey-roasted peanuts, for garnish
	6 metal skewers

Make Ahead

1. Season the pork with salt and pepper. Place in a bowl with the ½ cup peanut sauce and toss well to combine. Cover the bowl with plastic wrap and let stand at room temperature for 30 minutes or refrigerate up to overnight.

2. In a separate bowl, toss the pineapple chunks with the olive oil and season with salt and pepper.

3. Thread 3 to 5 chunks each of pork and pineapple onto the skewers, alternating between the two. Pack the skewers in tightly sealed plastic containers to transport in the cooler.

At the Game

1. Preheat the grill to medium-high heat and brush the grate with oil or spray with nonstick cooking spray.

2. Transfer the skewers to the grill. Close the cover and cook, turning once halfway through, until the pineapple is lightly caramelized and the pork is just cooked through, 3 to 4 minutes per side. Sprinkle with peanuts and serve with additional peanut sauce for dipping.

Gotta Be in It to Win It!

We have the most fun living by the tailgater's creed: We may not win the game, but we always win the party.

Pesto Shrimp Skewers

Not only are these pesto shrimp skewers as tasty as can be, they won't weigh you down before you do all that rooting for the home team. They're just the thing to serve when you know your stomach is about to be doing some flip-flops over a close score. These skewers are even better when you serve them with a light salad on the side. We like Lemon-Basil Green Bean Almondine Salad (page 151). **Serves 6**

¾ pound extra-large shrimp, peeled and
  deveined
4 ounces cherry tomatoes (about 1½ cups)
Salt and freshly ground black pepper

6 tablespoons prepared pesto sauce (found in the
  refrigerated section of the supermarket) or
  Homemade Pesto (page 11)

6 metal skewers

Make Ahead

1. Season the shrimp and tomatoes with salt and pepper. Place in a large bowl with the pesto sauce and toss well to combine. Cover the bowl with plastic wrap and let stand at room temperature for 30 minutes or refrigerate up to overnight.

2. Thread 3 to 5 each of shrimp and tomatoes onto the skewers, alternating between the two. Pack the skewers in tightly sealed plastic containers to transport in the cooler.

At the Game

1. Preheat the grill to high heat and brush the grate with oil or spray with nonstick cooking spray.

2. Transfer the skewers to the grill. Close the cover and cook, turning once halfway through, until the tomatoes are lightly charred and the shrimp are just cooked through, about 2 minutes per side.

Metal Conquers Wood

When it comes to grilling skewers, we always choose metal over wood. Though it means more cleanup, we think it makes more sense to clean and reuse more durable items rather than buy cheaper throwaway goods. It's better for the environment. And you don't have to worry about the metal catching on fire!

Party Chokes

These easy skewers can be counted on to get the party started. Ready in minutes, their simple preparation makes them a good fit for newbie grillers. We love to make these savory bites for tailgating, but, really, they're too much fun not to be on the menu anytime we fire up the grill.   **Serves 6**

One 12-ounce jar marinated whole artichoke hearts, drained
10 bacon strips, cut crosswise in half

4 to 6 metal skewers, depending on the length of the skewer

Make Ahead

1. Cut the artichokes into quarters. Wrap 1 cut bacon strip around each artichoke.

2. Thread 3 to 5 wrapped artichokes onto each skewer (poking the tip of the skewer through the overlapping ends of the bacon to secure). Pack the skewers in tightly sealed plastic containers to transport in the cooler.

At the Game

1. Preheat the grill to medium-high heat and brush the grate with oil or spray with nonstick cooking spray.

2. Place the skewers on the grill. Close the cover and cook, turning once halfway through, for 3 minutes.

3. Open the cover and continue to cook, turning occasionally, until the bacon is cooked through, 6 to 8 minutes.

Spicy Prosciutto-Wrapped Shrimp and Scallop Skewers

These seafood skewers make our parking lot table very popular with the rest of the tailgaters—they always seem to stop by for a neighborly hello just when we're taking the skewers off the grill. We don't mind. Sharing skewers is the name of the game when the home team plays. To make grilling a little simpler, we make the mayo-rosemary glaze at home and transport it in a resealable plastic bag. The seafood gets packed in separate plastic containers, too, and everything is set to be assembled on site. **Serves 6**

Pinch of salt, plus additional to taste
½ garlic clove, minced
¼ cup mayonnaise
1½ teaspoons chopped fresh rosemary
1 tablespoon olive oil
½ pound large shrimp, rinsed and patted dry

½ pound sea scallops, rinsed and patted dry
Freshly ground black pepper
¼ pound thinly sliced prosciutto, cut into
   1-inch-wide strips

6 metal skewers

Make Ahead

1. Add a pinch of salt to the garlic and, using a mortar and pestle or the flat part of a chef's knife, mash the mixture into a paste. Transfer the paste to a small bowl and stir in the mayonnaise, rosemary, and olive oil until combined.

2. Thread the shrimp and scallops onto the skewers and season with the additional salt and the pepper. Brush the seafood with the mayonnaise mixture. Wrap half the seafood with strips of prosciutto (leave the remaining half bare). Pack the skewers in tightly sealed plastic containers to transport in the cooler.

At the Game

1. Preheat the grill to medium-high heat and brush the grate with oil or spray with nonstick cooking spray.

2. Transfer the skewers to the grill. Close the cover and cook, turning once halfway through, until the seafood is just opaque and the prosciutto has crisped up, 1½ to 2 minutes per side.

Grilled Ham, Veggie, and Mozzarella Skewers

This is a perfect example of the beauty of a skewer—you've got a whole square meal right there in one hand. We love the way mozzarella cheese keeps its creaminess after grilling—without melting all over the place. It's the only cheese we'd dare skewer at our tailgating parties. And if you want to get a little more of that good and healthy green stuff into your system, serve these skewers with Broccoli Salad with Walnuts and Raisins (page 153). **Serves 6**

10 ounces thinly sliced deli ham	½ cup olive oil
One 8-ounce package mozzarella cheese, cut into 1½-inch chunks (about 2 cups)	Salt and freshly ground black pepper
6 ounces cherry tomatoes (about 2 cups)	6 metal skewers
5 ounces white mushrooms, halved if large	Grill basket
1 medium zucchini, cut into 1½-inch chunks	

Make Ahead

1. Cut the ham slices lengthwise into 2-inch-long strips. Wrap a strip of ham around each chunk of cheese.

2. Alternating with the cheese and vegetables, thread 2 or 3 chunks of ham-wrapped cheese, and some tomatoes, mushrooms, and zucchini onto each skewer. Pack the skewers in tightly sealed plastic containers to transport in the cooler.

At the Game

1. Preheat the grill to medium-high heat.

2. Brush the skewers generously with olive oil; season with salt and pepper.

3. Arrange the skewers in a grill basket. Place the basket on the grill. Close the cover and cook until the vegetables are golden and tender, about 2 minutes per side.

A Little Something Sweet MORE AND MORE S'MORES

Remember the classic s'mores we'd roast around the campfire when we were kids? They still delight, even when fixed up with slightly more sophisticated ingredients. **Serves 4**

8 graham cracker rectangles
8 ounces favorite milk or specialty chocolate, such as ginger, orange, or Mexican spiced
8 large marshmallows

1. Break the graham cracker rectangles in half to make 16 cracker squares. Break the chocolate into bite-size pieces. Cut the marshmallows in half.

2. Sandwich some chocolate and 2 marshmallow pieces between 2 crackers. Repeat with the remaining ingredients.

3. Preheat the grill to medium and place a sheet of heavy-duty aluminum foil on the grate.

4. Place the s'mores, marshmallow side down (to prevent the chocolate from oozing too much during cooking), on the foil. Close the cover and cook until the s'mores are gooey, about 3 minutes.

5

Burgers and Dawgs

Mexican Fiesta Burgers

Brooke and little Jack have always been big Mexican food fans, and we created these spicy burgers just for them. In keeping with the theme, we don't serve the burgers with ketchup—just sliced avocado, jalapeño pepper, and salsa on top. For a couple of salsas that are more special than the kinds you can buy in the store, try our Home-Baked Tortilla Chips with Two Kinds of Salsa (page 166). **Serves 8**

---

1 cup prepared salsa or homemade (see page 166), plus additional for serving

3 pounds ground beef

½ cup grated Monterey Jack cheese (2 ounces)

2 teaspoons salt

2 teaspoons freshly ground black pepper

8 hamburger buns

Sliced avocado, for serving

Thinly sliced fresh jalapeño pepper, for serving (optional)

Make Ahead

Strain the salsa through a sieve into a bowl, pressing down with a spoon to remove as much excess liquid as possible. In a bowl, mix together the salsa, ground beef, Monterey Jack cheese, salt, and pepper until just combined. Form the beef mixture into eight 1-inch-thick patties. Pack the patties into a plastic bag and place in the cooler to transport.

At the Game

1. Preheat the grill to medium-high heat and brush the grate with oil or spray with nonstick cooking spray.

2. Transfer the burgers to the grill. Close the cover and cook to the desired doneness, 3 to 5 minutes per side. Let the burgers rest off the grill while toasting the buns.

3. Meanwhile, place the buns on the grill, cut side down, until lightly toasted, about 1 minute.

4. Sandwich the burgers, additional salsa, avocado, and jalapeño (if using) inside the buns and serve.

Burgers Made to Order

On our picnic table, we set out three platters with labels for rare, medium-rare, and well-done. We slide the burgers off onto their corresponding platters as they're ready, and guests can help themselves to their favorite.

Bacon-and-Cheddar-Stuffed Burgers

This is not for everyday eating, but for extra-special cookouts where a normal grilled burger just won't do. As a once-in-a-while treat, this goodie-stuffed burger will set your world on fire—well worth eating a healthy salad such as Broccoli Salad with Walnuts and Raisins (page 153) for the rest of the week! **Serves 8**

16 slices cooked bacon, crumbled	1 teaspoon salt
1½ cups grated cheddar cheese (6 ounces)	1 teaspoon freshly ground black pepper
½ cup finely chopped red onion	8 hamburger buns
3 pounds ground beef	

Make Ahead

1. In a bowl, combine the bacon, cheddar cheese, and onion.

2. In a separate bowl, mix together the ground beef, salt, and pepper until just combined. Form the beef mixture into eight 1-inch-thick patties. Make a ¾-inch well in the center of each patty. Place about 1 tablespoon of the bacon-cheese mixture into each well and close the meat up around the filling (re-form into patties, if necessary). Pack the patties into a plastic bag and place in the cooler to transport.

At the Game

1. Preheat the grill to medium-high and brush the grate with oil or spray with nonstick cooking spray.

2. Transfer the burgers to the grill. Close the cover and cook to the desired doneness, 3 to 5 minutes per side. Let the burgers rest off the grill while toasting the buns.

3. Meanwhile, place the buns on the grill, cut side down, until lightly toasted, about 1 minute.

4. Sandwich the burgers inside the buns and serve with your favorite condiments.

TOP TIPS FOR THE BEST BURGERS

When it comes down to it, a good grilled burger is all about the meat. We like to use a blend of fatty ground chuck and leaner sirloin (at a ratio of about 80 to 20 percent), for a nice, juicy burger.

When forming the patty, handle the meat as little as possible. Start out by wetting your hands with a little water; this will keep the ground meat from sticking to your skin. Then gently pat the meat into a patty. Pressing the meat too tightly into a photogenic little puck will lead to a tough burger, and we'll take tenderness over picture-perfect beauty any day.

And when you set that patty on the grill, no matter how tempted you are by that sweet hiss of burger grease hitting the hot coals, never (and we mean never, ever) press the patty down with your spatula. Not only will this compact and toughen the meat, it will squeeze out all those fantastic juices—burger juice belongs in the bun, not lost on the grill!

Portabello Pesto Burgers

Grilled burgers mixed with our fantastic basil pesto are such a treat and have become a mainstay at our family cookouts. Portabello mushrooms really take in that smoky cookout flavor and are an excellent topper—sometimes we melt a little mozzarella cheese on top of it all, but sometimes we just want the flavors of mushroom, beef, and pesto. Either way, we know you'll make these again and again. **Serves 8**

4 portabello mushroom caps (about ¾ pound)
¼ cup olive oil, plus additional for brushing
1 teaspoon salt, plus additional to taste
1 teaspoon freshly ground black pepper,
    plus additional to taste
3 pounds ground beef
1 cup prepared pesto (found in the refrigerated
    section of the supermarket) or Homemade
    Pesto (page 11)

8 hamburger buns
6 ounces mozzarella cheese, thickly sliced,
    for serving (optional)

Grill basket (optional)

Make Ahead

1. In a bowl, gently toss the mushroom caps with the olive oil and the additional salt and pepper to taste. Pack the mushrooms into a plastic bag and place in the cooler to transport.

2. In a separate bowl, mix together the ground beef, ½ cup of the pesto, and the 1 teaspoon each of salt and pepper until just combined. Form the beef mixture into eight 1-inch-thick patties. Pack the patties into a plastic bag and place in the cooler to transport.

At the Game

1. Preheat the grill to medium-high heat and brush the grate with oil or spray with nonstick cooking spray.

2. Arrange the mushrooms in a single layer on the grill (or in a grill basket). Close the cover and cook until the mushrooms are tender and juicy, 2 to 3 minutes per side. Transfer the mushrooms to a plate and cover with aluminum foil to keep warm.

3. Place the burgers on the grill. Close the cover and cook to the desired doneness, 3 to 5 minutes per side. Let the burgers rest off the grill while toasting the buns.

4. Meanwhile, place the buns on the grill, cut side down, until lightly toasted, about 1 minute.

5. Thinly slice the mushrooms. If using the mozzarella cheese, place it on the burgers and transfer the burgers to the upper rack of the grill or away from the direct heat until the cheese melts, 1 to 2 minutes.

6. Sandwich the burgers, mushrooms, and the remaining pesto inside the buns and serve.

Ultimate Onion Burgers

Here in the South we love our sweet Vidalia onions (Georgia's state vegetable) so much that we just had to create a whole burger in their honor. Trust us, if you love onions, you are going to go wild for these burgers. A word to the wise: Make sure you pass around the breath mints when you're finished! **Serves 8**

2 medium Vidalia onions, cut into ½-inch-thick rounds

2 tablespoons olive oil

1 teaspoon salt, plus additional to taste

1 teaspoon freshly ground black pepper, plus additional to taste

3 pounds ground beef

¼ cup chopped scallions (white and light green parts)

One 1- to 2-ounce envelope onion soup and dip mix

8 hamburger buns

Grill basket

Make Ahead

1. Brush the onions with the olive oil and season with the additional salt and pepper to taste. Pack the onions into a plastic bag and place in the cooler to transport.

2. In a bowl, mix together the ground beef, scallions, soup mix, and the 1 teaspoon each of salt and pepper until just combined. Form the beef mixture into eight 1-inch-thick patties. Pack the patties into a plastic bag and place in the cooler to transport.

At the Game

1. Preheat the grill to medium-high heat and brush the grate with oil or spray with nonstick cooking spray.

2. Place the onions in a grill basket. Transfer the basket to the grill. Close the cover and cook until tender and charred, about 5 minutes per side.

3. Transfer the burgers to the grill. Close the cover and cook to the desired doneness, 3 to 5 minutes per side. Let the burgers rest off the grill while you toast the buns.

4. Meanwhile, place the buns on the grill, cut side down, until lightly toasted, about 1 minute.

5. Sandwich the burgers and grilled onions inside the buns and serve.

Steak House Burgers

Back when we were both bachelors, we used to have brothers' nights out that often started at the steak house with a double order of onion rings and T-bone steaks. Well, these burgers, loaded with garlic, steak sauce, and topped with our favorite onion rings, are even better. Not only do we get to enjoy them in the comfort of our own backyards (or served out of the back of our car at tailgating parties), but Brooke, Jack, Mama, Michael, and the rest of the group are in on the fun! **Serves 8**

3 pounds ground beef	**2 teaspoons salt**
4 tablespoons (½ stick) frozen unsalted butter, grated	**8 large prepared frozen onion rings**
2 large garlic cloves, finely chopped	**1 cup steak sauce**
1 tablespoon coarsely ground black pepper	**8 hamburger buns**
	8 tomato slices, for serving

Make Ahead

In a bowl, mix together the ground beef, butter, garlic, pepper, and salt until just combined. Form the beef mixture into eight 1-inch-thick patties. Pack the patties into a plastic bag and place in the cooler to transport.

At the Game

1. Preheat the grill to medium-high heat and brush the grate with oil or spray with nonstick cooking spray.

2. Place the onion rings on the grill. Close the cover and cook until crisp and golden, 2 to 3 minutes per side. Transfer the onion rings to a plate.

3. Place ½ cup of the steak sauce in a small bowl and brush each burger with steak sauce. Transfer the burgers to the grill. Close the cover and cook, brushing halfway through with more steak sauce, to the desired doneness, 3 to 5 minutes per side. Place the buns on the grill, cut side down, for the last minute of cooking and toast lightly.

4. Place the remaining steak sauce in a separate bowl and, using a clean brush, brush the burgers with additional steak sauce and sandwich the burgers, onion rings, and tomato slices inside the buns and serve.

Hot Buffalo Burgers with Blue Cheese

Inspired by hot Buffalo wings, these beef burgers have the same great game-day flavor, but are much easier to eat. If you're like Jamie and want your burger nuclear hot, add an extra dash of Tabasco to the mayo—and mix up a pitcher of Frosty Piña Colada Punch (page 194) to cool yourself down. **Serves 8**

½ cup crumbled blue cheese (2 ounces)	2 teaspoons salt
¼ cup mayonnaise	2 teaspoons freshly ground black pepper
8 tablespoons (1 stick) unsalted butter, melted	8 hamburger buns
5 tablespoons Tabasco or other hot sauce	2 small Vidalia onions, cut into ¼-inch-thick rounds
3 pounds ground beef	½ cup chopped celery leaves

Make Ahead

1. In a small bowl, stir together the blue cheese and mayonnaise.

2. In a separate bowl, whisk together the butter and 2½ tablespoons of the Tabasco.

3. In another bowl, mix together the ground beef, the remaining 2½ tablespoons Tabasco, the salt, and pepper until just combined. Form the beef mixture into eight 1-inch-thick patties and brush with some of the Tabasco butter. Pack the patties into a plastic bag and place in the cooler to transport.

At the Game

1. Preheat the grill to medium-high heat and brush the grate with oil or spray with nonstick cooking spray.

2. Transfer the burgers to the grill. Close the cover and cook, brushing halfway through with more Tabasco butter, to the desired doneness, 3 to 5 minutes per side. Let the burgers rest off the grill while toasting the buns.

3. Meanwhile, place the buns on the grill, cut side down, until lightly toasted, about 1 minute.

4. Brush the burgers with additional Tabasco butter. Sandwich the onion slices, celery leaves, and a dollop of blue cheese dressing inside the buns and serve.

Spicy Asian Tuna Burgers

This is a great way to get a little more tuna (with its mega-healthy omega-3 fatty acids) into your diet. The Asian-inspired flavor wows whenever we grill these tuna burgers. They may be a little too sophisticated for the kids, but the grown-ups eat 'em up. **Serves 8**

3 pounds yellowfin tuna, diced	**2½ tablespoons grated fresh ginger**
½ cup soy sauce	**Peanut or vegetable oil, for brushing**
½ cup chopped scallions (white and light green parts)	**8 hamburger buns**
¼ cup toasted sesame oil	**½ cup prepared peanut sauce**
	Sliced tomatoes, for serving

Make Ahead

Place the tuna, soy sauce, scallions, sesame oil, and ginger in a food processor; pulse a few times until roughly chopped (do not overprocess). Form the tuna mixture into eight 1-inch-thick patties, pressing together tightly to bind. Brush the patties generously with peanut oil. Pack the patties into a plastic bag and place in the cooler to transport.

At the Game

1. Preheat the grill to medium-high heat and brush the grate with oil or spray with nonstick cooking spray.

2. Transfer the burgers to the grill. Close the cover and cook until just cooked through, 3 to 5 minutes. Place the buns on the grill, cut side down, for the last minute of cooking and toast lightly.

3. Sandwich the burgers, peanut sauce, and tomato slices inside the buns and serve.

Tip

Don't Forget the H_2O!

Bring an extra two gallons of water for putting out hot coals. You can always spot rookie tailgaters: They're the ones trying to douse their grills with Pomegranate Punch (page 194).

Bobby's Turkey Burgers with Hummus

Bobby is definitely the healthier brother, but he does not live on salad alone. When he's the grill master, his famous turkey burgers are on the menu—and he never hears any complaints! Yummy hummus spread on top really perks up the taste buds—healthy never tasted so good! **Serves 8**

3 pounds ground turkey	**½ cup prepared hummus (found in the refrigerated**
2 teaspoons salt	**section of the supermarket)**
2 teaspoons freshly ground black pepper	**Sliced tomatoes, for serving**
2 teaspoons ground cumin	**Shredded lettuce, for serving**
¼ teaspoon cayenne pepper	**Sliced onions, for serving**
8 hamburger buns	

Make Ahead

In a bowl, mix together the turkey, salt, black pepper, cumin, and cayenne until just combined. Form the turkey mixture into eight 1-inch-thick patties. Pack the patties into a plastic bag and place in the cooler to transport.

At the Game

1. Preheat the grill to medium-high heat and brush the grate with oil or spray with nonstick cooking spray.

2. Transfer the burgers to the grill. Close the cover and cook until cooked through, about 5 minutes per side. Let the burgers rest off the grill while toasting the buns.

3. Meanwhile, place the buns on the grill, cut side down, until lightly toasted, about 1 minute.

4. Sandwich the burgers inside the buns along with a dollop of hummus, some tomato slices, lettuce, and onions and serve.

Beer Brats on the Grill

This recipe comes courtesy of our good buddy Luke Zei, who is originally from Green Bay, Wisconsin (Go, Pack!). It's a fantastic preparation when you're tailgating with a big crowd. There's no need to make anything in advance; it can all be done at the game. Give the brats a nice char over the flame after they've been soaking in the brew, and we guarantee the first one you grill will be every bit as tasty and juicy as the last. Plus, you get to enjoy the sixth beer yourself as a grill master's treat. You can't beat that! **Serves 4**

One 14-ounce package precooked bratwurst (4 brats)
Six 12-ounce lager beers
1 large yellow onion, cut into ¼-inch-thick rounds
4 hot dog buns

Sauerkraut, for serving
Mustard, for serving

Two 9 x 13-inch aluminum roasting pans (3 inches deep)

At the Game

1. Prick the bratwurst all over with a fork and set aside.

2. Place one roasting pan inside the other to make a sturdy, double-thick pan that will securely contain the liquid and brats. Pour 5 beers into the pan (save the sixth for drinking later by the grill). Stir in the onions.

3. Preheat the grill to high heat and brush the grate with oil or spray with nonstick cooking spray.

4. Transfer the roasting pans to the grill. Close the cover and bring the liquid to a simmer (this will take about 15 minutes). Add the brats to the pan and continue to simmer for 25 minutes. Using pot holders, carefully remove the pan from the grill.

5. Brush the grate with oil or spray with nonstick cooking spray. Reduce the heat to medium-high.

6. Using tongs, transfer the brats to the grill. Close the cover and cook, turning occasionally, until the brats are golden, about 5 minutes. Place the buns on the grill, cut side down, for the last minute of cooking and toast lightly.

7. Sandwich the brats inside the buns. Top the brats with the sauerkraut and mustard.

Red Dawgs

This is what you'll find us grilling on UGA game days! Don't forget to grill the buns; it's a small touch that adds so much to a grilled dog. And be sure to get creative with the fixings. We love spicy mustard, mayo, and pickles. These juicy dogs will get you fired up with team spirit—Go, Dawgs! **Serves 8**

3 tablespoons ketchup

2 tablespoons light brown sugar

½ teaspoon Tabasco or other hot sauce

One 16-ounce package hot dogs (8 dogs)

8 hot dog buns

Make Ahead

In a small saucepan over medium heat, stir together the ketchup, brown sugar, and Tabasco. Cook until the brown sugar is completely dissolved, about 3 minutes. Brush the hot dogs generously with the glaze. Pack the dogs into a plastic bag and place in the cooler to transport.

At the Game

1. Preheat the grill to medium-high heat and brush the grate with oil or spray with nonstick cooking spray.

2. Transfer the hot dogs to the grill. Close the cover and cook, turning occasionally, until the dogs are golden all over, about 5 minutes. Place the buns on the grill, cut side down, for the last minute of cooking and toast lightly.

3. Sandwich the hot dogs inside the buns and top them with your favorite condiments.

Good Doggies

Aka "the Bobby special." Because going all out with the hot dog fixings doesn't mean you have to leave your healthy eating habits behind. Bring all the fixings with you to the game and you can make these right there in the parking lot. Turkey bacon, fresh onion, and crunchy shredded lettuce make for a guilt-free (Bobby-approved) tailgating treat. **Serves 8**

One 16-ounce package hot dogs (8 dogs)	**½ cup Boursin Light cheese**
8 slices turkey bacon	**6 tablespoons finely chopped onion, for serving**
Olive oil, for brushing	**Shredded lettuce, for serving**
8 hot dog buns	

At the Game

1. Preheat the grill to medium-high heat and brush the grate with oil or spray with nonstick cooking spray.

2. Wrap each hot dog in a bacon slice, spiraling the bacon around the dog lengthwise. Brush each lightly with olive oil.

3. Transfer the hot dogs to the grill. Close the cover and cook, turning occasionally, until the bacon is crisp and the hot dogs are slightly charred, 3 to 5 minutes. Transfer to a plate while toasting the buns.

4. Place the buns on the grill, cut side down, until light golden, about 1 minute.

5. Reduce the heat to medium. Spread the buns with the Boursin cheese and place on the upper rack of the grill or away from the direct heat for 1 minute to warm through.

6. Sandwich the hot dogs inside the buns. Sprinkle each dog with onion and lettuce and serve.

Bad Doggies

Then again, if you're like Jamie, sometimes you just gotta be a little devilish with your dogs. Stuffed with chipotle in adobo sauce (that'll put the hot in your dog!), wrapped in bacon, and sprinkled with cheddar cheese, these dogs make being bad taste oh so good. **Serves 8**

One 16-ounce package hot dogs (8 dogs)
¼ cup canned chipotle chile in adobo sauce, seeded, if desired, and minced
8 slices bacon

8 hot dog buns
2 cups grated cheddar cheese (8 ounces)
6 tablespoons finely chopped onion, for serving

At the Game

1. Split each hot dog lengthwise with a sharp knife (do not cut all the way through). Fill each with a layer of chipotle. Press the halves closed. Wrap each hot dog in a bacon slice, spiraling the bacon lengthwise around the dog.

2. Preheat the grill to medium-high heat and brush the grate with oil or spray with nonstick cooking spray.

3. Transfer the hot dogs to the grill. Close the cover and cook, turning occasionally, until the bacon is crisp and the hot dogs are slightly charred, about 5 minutes. Transfer to a plate while toasting the buns.

4. Place the buns on the grill, cut side down, until lightly toasted, about 1 minute.

5. Reduce the heat to medium. Sprinkle the buns with the cheddar cheese and place on the upper rack of the grill or away from the direct heat. Close the cover and cook until the cheese is melted, about 2 minutes.

6. Sandwich the hot dogs inside the bun. Sprinkle each dog with onion and serve.

A Little Something Sweet
GRILLED CHOCOLATE AND HEATH BAR QUESADILLAS

Sometimes you need an extra little rush of sugar right before you douse the fire and head into the stadium. There is no better way to get it than in these chocolaty-toffee tortillas done quesadilla style on the grill. For a coconut variation, substitute ½ cup shredded coconut for the chopped Heath bar.
Serves 4

Eight 8-inch flour tortillas
½ cup milk chocolate chips
½ cup chopped Heath bar
Melted butter, for brushing

   1. Arrange the tortillas on a clean work surface. Sprinkle 4 of the tortillas with 2 tablespoons each milk chocolate chips and chopped Heath bar. Top with the remaining 4 tortillas. Brush the tops and bottoms of the tortillas with the melted butter.

   2. Preheat the grill to medium-high heat and brush the grate with oil or spray with nonstick cooking spray.

   3. Place the quesadillas on the grill. Close the cover and cook until the chocolate is melted and the tortillas are golden brown, 1 to 1½ minutes per side.

6

Snacks, Sides, and Pregame Bites

Game Day Breakfast to Go

Some mornings you're so anxious to get on the road that you don't want to waste time sitting down to breakfast. Our solution is to get these breakfasts to go ready the night before the big game. Just pop 'em in the oven as you're getting ready to leave—20 minutes later you can wrap them in a napkin and enjoy them on the way to the stadium. We usually make them with sliced deli ham, but we sometimes mix it up with cooked crumbled sausage or bacon or sub in grated pepper Jack cheese for the cheddar. Any way you like them, your hunger satisfied, no time lost, you're already starting out a winner! **Serves 10**

One 12-ounce can refrigerated buttermilk biscuits (10 biscuits)

3 large eggs

½ teaspoon salt

½ teaspoon freshly ground black pepper

⅓ pound sliced deli ham, diced

½ cup plus 2 tablespoons grated cheddar cheese

1. Preheat the oven to 350°F. Generously grease a 12-cup muffin pan.

2. Using a sharp knife, slice each round of biscuit dough in half horizontally (making 2 rounds) and place 1 round in each of 10 muffin cups.

3. In a bowl, whisk together the eggs, salt, and pepper.

4. Sprinkle the ham evenly over the biscuit rounds in the muffin cups. Spoon about 2 tablespoons of the egg mixture over the ham, dividing it evenly among the muffin cups. Top with the ½ cup cheddar cheese and cover each muffin cup with a remaining biscuit round. Sprinkle the remaining cheese on the biscuit tops. Fill the 2 empty muffin cups halfway with water to prevent scorching.

5. Bake until the biscuits are golden and firm and the egg is cooked through, about 20 minutes. Let cool slightly. Use an offset spatula to loosen the edges of the biscuits and pop the biscuits out of the pan. Serve immediately or let cool completely and wrap in aluminum foil for on-the-go snacking.

Make a List and Check It Twice!

In sports and in life there are times that call for spontaneity and times that call for planning ahead—and tailgating definitely calls for planning ahead! Make a list the night before that includes what supplies you need to take with you (and don't forget little things like paper towels, a grilling mitt, and, oh yeah, your tickets to the game). Check the items off as you load them into the car to guarantee a winning day.

Savannah Tailgater Chili

There is nothing like a belly full of hot chili to steady a fan before watching a big game. We make ours at home the day before, load it up with spices and all the good stuff, and heat it over the grill when we tailgate. You can also try toting some of it to the game in a couple of thermoses. It is a full meal in a bowl; we couldn't get through the Dawgs season without it. **Serves 6 to 8**

3 tablespoons olive oil

2 pounds ground beef

2½ teaspoons kosher salt

½ teaspoon freshly ground black pepper

1 medium onion, diced (about 1 cup)

1 small green bell pepper, seeded and diced (about ½ cup)

2 large garlic cloves, finely chopped

¼ cup chili powder, plus additional to taste

2 teaspoons dried oregano

1½ teaspoons ground cumin

Three 15-ounce cans red kidney beans, drained and rinsed

One 28-ounce can diced tomatoes

One 15-ounce can tomato sauce

One 10-ounce bag frozen corn kernels

Sour cream, for serving

Grated cheddar cheese, for serving

1. Heat 2 tablespoons of the olive oil in a large pot over medium-high heat. Brown the ground beef, breaking it up with a fork, until cooked through, 7 to 8 minutes. Season with ½ teaspoon of the salt and the pepper. Using a slotted spoon, transfer the beef to a paper-towel-lined plate to drain.

2. Heat the remaining 1 tablespoon olive oil in the pot. Add the onion, bell pepper, and garlic and sauté until softened, about 5 minutes. Stir in the chili powder, oregano, and cumin and cook for 1 minute.

3. Return the beef to the pot. Stir in the beans, tomatoes, tomato sauce, corn, 1½ cups water, and the remaining 2 teaspoons salt. Simmer for 30 minutes. Taste and add more chili powder, if desired.

4. Ladle the chili into bowls and top with a dollop of sour cream and a sprinkling of cheddar cheese to serve.

Grilled Stuffed Corn Bread with Ham and Cheese

These buttery, cheesy, peppery sandwiches are a mighty fine way to use up leftover corn bread. We make each square about two bites' worth in size, just right to slake our appetite until the burgers and dogs come off the grill. These are great served alongside any of our skewers, especially Meat 'n' Potato Skewers (page 83) or Italian Chicken and Tricolor Peppers Skewers (page 84). **Serves 4**

---

1 pound corn bread
2 teaspoons Dijon mustard
¼ pound thinly sliced deli ham
¼ pound thinly sliced cheese of your choice

8 small hot pickled peppers, such as peperoncini, halved lengthwise
4 tablespoons (½ stick) unsalted butter, melted

Make Ahead

1. Cut the corn bread into ½-inch slices.

2. Spread each slice with mustard and sandwich the ham, cheese, and pickled peppers between 2 slices of corn bread. Repeat with the remaining corn bread, ham, cheese, and pickled peppers. Wrap the corn bread squares in aluminum foil. Pack the foil packets into the cooler to transport.

At the Game

1. Preheat the grill to medium heat and brush the grate with oil or spray with nonstick cooking spray.

2. Brush both sides of each "sandwich" with the butter. Transfer the sandwiches to the grill. Close the cover and cook until the cheese is melted and the corn bread is toasted, 2 to 3 minutes per side.

Chili-Topped Overstuffed Potatoes

Take our famous Savannah Tailgater Chili right up to the next level when you serve it in an edible bowl!
Serves 4

4 russet potatoes	½ teaspoon salt
½ cup sour cream	1 cup Savannah Tailgater Chili (page 114) or prepared chili
2 tablespoons unsalted butter, cut into pieces	
1 teaspoon freshly ground black pepper	Chopped scallions, for garnish

Make Ahead

1. Preheat the oven to 400°F.

2. To bake the potatoes, prick each all over with a fork, wrap individually in aluminum foil (this will make it easier to transport later, when the potatoes are stuffed with chili), and bake until tender, about 1 hour.

3. While the potatoes are hot, carefully unwrap the foil and reserve. Horizontally slice off the top quarter of each, reserving the lids. Using a spoon, scoop out the potato insides into a bowl, leaving a ¼-inch border and the skin intact.

4. Mash the potato insides with the sour cream, butter, pepper, and salt. Return the filling to the potato skins.

5. Place the potatoes on the reserved squares of aluminum foil. Spoon the chili over each potato and cover with the reserved potato lid. Loosely close the sides of the foil into packets. Pack the foil packets into the cooler to transport.

At the Game

1. Preheat the grill to medium-high heat.

2. Transfer the potato packets to the grill. Close the cover and cook until heated through, 8 to 10 minutes. Unwrap the potatoes and garnish with the scallions to serve.

Creamy Ham and Pickle Roll-Ups

Make these snacks ahead and pack 'em in the cooler to enjoy while the grill heats up. Sour pickle lovers will not be able to get enough of these creamy treats. We just love how these pickles taste right alongside our Red Dawgs (page 107)! **Serves 8**

One 8-ounce package cream cheese, softened	**1 pound thinly sliced deli ham**
3 tablespoons chopped fresh dill	**16 dill pickle spears**

1. In a small bowl, mash together the cream cheese and dill.
2. Spread each slice of ham with the cream cheese mixture. Top with a pickle spear and roll up.

Extra-Big Game? Make an Extra-Big Batch!

We often make double batches of tailgating finger foods like Creamy Ham and Pickle Roll-Ups (see above) and Pickled Okra Stuffed with Scallion Cream Cheese (page 122) whenever there's an especially big game on the day's roster. Our reasoning is simple: Big games can mean big traffic jams, and nobody likes to sit in the car with a growling stomach.

Tailgater's Vidalia BLT

We love doing bacon on the grill, so it was a natural that we'd make some BLTs. You can make these awesome sammies at the game—no need for advance preparation here. Sweet Vidalia onions are a must at any Georgia game, though we're willing to bet they'll go over big at any arena. Maybe not at a Florida Gators game, but that's another story. **Serves 6**

Two 2-ounce packages ready-to-serve sliced bacon, such as Oscar Mayer
Twelve ½-inch-thick slices good-quality white bread

6 tablespoons mayonnaise
2 medium tomatoes, cut into ¼-inch-thick slices
1 Vidalia onion, thinly sliced
1½ cups shredded iceberg or Boston lettuce

1. Preheat the grill to medium-high heat and brush the grate with oil or spray with nonstick cooking spray.

2. Place the bacon strips on the grill and cook, uncovered, until crisped, 30 seconds to 1 minute per side. Transfer to a paper-towel-lined plate.

3. Place the bread on the grill. Close the cover and cook until lightly toasted, about 1 minute per side.

4. Spread each slice of toast with mayonnaise. Sandwich the bacon, tomatoes, onion, and lettuce between toast slices.

Pickled Okra Stuffed with Scallion Cream Cheese

We grew up snacking on pickled okra and could polish off a whole jar before you could say, "Go, Dawgs." Believe it or not, the okra tastes even better stuffed with scallion cream cheese. Make these the night before; wrap in aluminum foil or place in a plastic bag and pack into the cooler, to have one less thing to check off your list on game day.   **Makes about 24 pieces**

One 16-ounce jar pickled okra	**2 tablespoons finely chopped scallions**
4 ounces cream cheese, softened	

1. Rinse the okra under running water and pat dry. Slice each okra in half lengthwise.

2. In a small bowl, mix the cream cheese and scallions together.

3. Sandwich the cream cheese mixture between 2 slices of okra. Serve immediately or wrap up and chill in the cooler until ready to serve.

Nutty Pimiento Cheese Balls

Bite-size pimiento cheese balls are a huge hit with all the kids. They're fun to make and even more fun to eat, perfect to keep tiny hands occupied while you're busy firing up the grill. Make sure you set some aside for the grill master. These cheese balls are good—and are just the thing to munch on with Pomegranate Punch (page 194)! **Makes about 3½ dozen balls**

2 ounces cream cheese, softened	1 teaspoon grated onion
2 cups grated sharp cheddar cheese (8 ounces)	⅛ teaspoon garlic powder
2 cups grated Monterey Jack cheese (8 ounces)	Pinch of salt
3 tablespoons mayonnaise	Pinch of freshly ground black pepper
3 tablespoons chopped pimiento	1½ cups chopped toasted pecans

1. Process the cream cheese in the bowl of a food processor until smooth. Add the cheddar cheese, Monterey Jack cheese, mayonnaise, pimiento, onion, garlic powder, salt, and pepper and pulse to combine. Scrape the cheese mixture into a bowl, cover, and refrigerate for 30 minutes or up to 2 days.

2. Place the pecans in a small bowl. Roll the cheese mixture into 1-inch balls and coat each ball evenly with the pecans.

3. Serve the cheese balls immediately or wrap them in plastic wrap and chill in the cooler until ready to serve.

A Little Something Sweet BOY SCOUT APPLES

We learned how to make these baked apples in Boy Scout sleepaway camp and still love to make them today! **Serves 4**

4 baking apples, such as Golden Delicious
4 tablespoons (½ stick) unsalted butter, softened
2 tablespoons sugar or raspberry jam
2 teaspoons ground cinnamon
⅛ teaspoon salt

   1. Core the apples and peel off a strip of skin around the equator of each apple to prevent bursting.

   2. In a small bowl, mash together the butter, sugar or raspberry jam, ground cinnamon, and salt. Fill each apple cavity with some of the mixture and wrap each apple individually in aluminum foil.

   3. Preheat a grill to medium-high heat.

   4. Place the apple packets on the grill. Close the cover and cook until the fruit is just tender, 8 to 10 minutes.

On the Blanket

Whether you're on a hiking trip or at an outdoor concert, there are times when eating outside means doing all your preparation in advance, so that when you get there you can just lay out your picnic blanket and relax. We have fond memories of the times we went up to the Tennessee mountains as kids to see the leaves change in the fall and just have some fun in that good mountain air. And it was always more affordable for us as a family to pack a cooler back at the house before we left instead of stopping at a restaurant or a fast food place on the way. As soon as we pulled out of the driveway, we'd be glued to the car windows, keeping our eyes peeled for the most scenic spot to pull up to and eat from that cooler as soon as we could.

Back then, we were all about sandwiches, and that sure hasn't changed. The sandwich was invented for portable, plate-free eating, but down here in the South . . . well, if you're having a Southern sandwich, you probably will need a plate. And you might need a fork, too. And you're definitely going to need plenty of napkins. (At least you will if we're packing your picnic!) The Deens don't do dry, thin little sandwiches. We do a simple **Red-Hot Mayo and Tomato Sandwich** (page 136) that is so delicious you won't care if it ends up on your pants—it'll be worth it. We also do some **Ham and Chutney Hungry Brothers Biscuits** (page 132) that are about as dainty as Jamie's bulldog, Champ. And let's just say that he is not the kind of dog you carry around in your purse, for several reasons.

We have sandwiches to thank for so much in our lives that it's no surprise we take them seriously. When Mama pulled herself out of the darkest time in her life, it was to start her first food business, a lunch delivery service called The Bag Lady. We were the ones delivering sandwiches from office to office, while Mama was back home making them. We knew they were the best sandwiches anyone in those offices had ever had, so we were determined to keep showing up until folks started to try them. The rest, as we say, is history—and it's why we believe in taking the time to make a truly spectacular sandwich, whether that means adding grated carrots and kalamata olives to our **Tuna Salad Wheels** (page 142) or mixing up some fiery avocado salsa for the best **Turkey and Pepper Jack Sammies with Chunky Avocado Salsa** (page 140) you've ever had.

Jamie will add **Classic Southern Slaw** (page 149) to any sandwich (or hot dog, but that's another chapter). In fact, a dollop of any salad is a great way to dress up a sandwich. But that's not the only reason to bring salads on a picnic. We love to have something crunchy and refreshing to eat on a warm afternoon, and salads add colorful zest to the meal. A well-sealed container full of our **Mediterranean Orzo Salad with Olives, Sun-Dried Tomatoes, and Pine Nuts** (page 146) or **NOLA-Style Dirty Rice Salad** (page 156) will round out a picnic perfectly, or it can be the main event of a lighter lunch.

Pretty salads, like an orange and green **Layered Mandarin Orange Salad** (page 152) or a fresh-tasting **Lemon-Basil Green Bean Almondine Salad** (page 151), just beg for a clear covered bowl or container so that you can enjoy looking at them. Whatever salad you pack, take the traveling time into account. We love a well-dressed salad where the flavors have had time to mingle, so we don't mind mixing everything together a few hours before serving time. But if you're packing the night before, or if you prefer perfectly crisp, lightly dressed leaves, pack up your dressing separately and mix when ready to serve. Croutons are best added right before serving, too. But most of the salads in this chapter will just get better as they sit. That's the beauty of our favorite dressing ingredient: good old mayonnaise.

Living in Savannah as we now do, there are plenty of occasions to picnic. We have beautiful parks downtown, and of course the Savannah Symphony plays the Picnic in the Park each year, when a lot of folks will get really serious about their picnic and bring out tables and chairs and candelabras and the whole deal. For occasions like these, we make our **Red Deviled Eggs** (page 163). They get their color and zing from ketchup and pimientos and are one of the picnic foods we do like to pack separately to keep fresh, then easily fill right before serving. They're a perfect way to start the meal because they're satisfying, fun to eat, popular with all ages, and just elegant enough to remind everyone that a picnic is a special meal.

Snacks are key whenever you're serving people of all ages or just sitting around on blankets for a good long afternoon. If folks are getting up to play ball, they're going to be that much hungrier, and bowls of **Home-Baked Tortilla Chips with Two Kinds of Salsa** (Green Tomato and Fresh Pineapple; page 166) or our **Georgia Caviar** (a kind of spicy bean dip; page 164) are always a welcome sight. And we figure, if you're relaxing out on the grass all afternoon, you might as well graze!

7

Sandwiches and Wraps on the Go

Ham and Chutney Hungry Brothers Biscuits

Biscuits and ham are a natural pair anywhere, but it's the duo of mustard and tangy mango chutney that really makes this sandwich something special. Add thinly sliced Vidalia onion to make it a real Southern treat—and serve with Georgia Peach Punch (page 199), of course. **Serves 8**

One 16.3-ounce can jumbo refrigerated buttermilk biscuits (8 biscuits)
⅓ cup unsalted butter, softened
1½ tablespoons Dijon mustard

1 pound thinly sliced Virginia ham
⅓ cup mango chutney
Sliced Vidalia or red onion (optional)

---

1. Bake the biscuits according to the package directions. Let the biscuits cool slightly, then split them in half horizontally.

2. Spread the cut side of each biscuit half with the butter and mustard. Sandwich the ham, chutney, and onion between the biscuit halves.

Keep a Picnic Kit

Every time you stop at a fast food joint ('fess up—we all do it sometimes), save the individual packets of ketchup, mustard, mayo, even salt and pepper. They're the perfect size to keep in your picnic basket condiment kit.

Pulled BBQ Chicken Sandwiches

So many supermarkets are selling rotisserie chicken these days that they make it much easier to get a classic Southern sandwich anytime you want it. Wrap each sandwich tightly in a paper napkin to keep the filling from spilling out. Or you can use this delicious sammie as a good opportunity to chill out and embrace the mess. And, as always, nothing completes a good Southern-style sammie like Classic Southern Slaw.

Serves 4

One 3-pound rotisserie chicken

1½ cups prepared barbecue sauce or homemade barbecue sauce (see page 10)

Classic Southern Slaw (page 149) or prepared coleslaw, for serving

Bread-and-butter pickles, for serving (optional)

4 kaiser rolls, split

1. Using your hands or a fork, shred the meat from the chicken, discarding the skin. (You should have about 2½ cups.)

2. In a large bowl, stir together the chicken and barbecue sauce. Sandwich the chicken mixture, slaw, and pickles between each split roll and serve.

Red-Hot Mayo and Tomato Sandwiches

A mayonnaise and tomato sandwich is a Southern staple. We think a little heat makes it all the more appetizing. And it makes a nice partner to some NOLA-Style Dirty Rice Salad (page 156). **Serves 6**

¾ cup mayonnaise

1 tablespoon Tabasco or other hot sauce, or to taste

⅛ teaspoon cayenne pepper

12 slices good-quality white bread

1 medium red onion, thinly sliced

2 large ripe tomatoes, cut crosswise into ¼-inch-thick slices

Salt and freshly ground black pepper

1. In a small bowl, whisk together the mayonnaise, Tabasco, and cayenne.

2. Spread the mayonnaise mixture over one side of each slice of bread. Arrange the onion on 6 slices and top with the tomatoes. Season with salt and pepper. Top with the remaining slices of bread and serve.

First Rule of Summer? Never Put a Tomato in the Fridge

Here in Savannah, our hot summers make our tomatoes extra juicy and sweet; we sometimes eat them up like apples. But no matter where you live, you want to hang on to every bit of flavorful juice in that fresh tomato by keeping it in a cool, dry place like the pantry, or even in a bowl on the table. Never, *ever* store it in the refrigerator. The fridge will destroy a tomato's texture, making it dry, chalky, and flavorless, a real crime against one of our favorite summertime flavors.

Bacon and Egg Salad Sandwiches

The salty crunch of crumbled bacon makes this one for the sandwich hall of fame. For optimum crunchiness, we recommend toasting the bread and assembling the sandwich at the picnic site. **Serves 4**

8 hard-boiled eggs, peeled and chopped
4 slices cooked bacon, crumbled
½ cup mayonnaise
4 scallions (white and light green parts), chopped
1 tablespoon **D**ijon mustard

½ teaspoon kosher salt
½ teaspoon freshly ground black pepper
8 slices good-quality white bread, toasted,
  if desired

1. In a large bowl, combine the eggs, bacon, mayonnaise, scallions, mustard, salt, and pepper.

2. Sandwich the egg salad between the bread slices and serve.

Bobby's Healthy Almond-Banana Sandwiches

When we were kids, we'd always beg Mama to fry us up some peanut butter and banana sandwiches. Now that we're (a little) older and (a little) wiser, we substitute heart-healthy almond butter and skip the frying pan. With a sprinkle of cinnamon sugar, the sandwich is still a pleasure—but not a guilty one. Kids will love this picnic treat as well. **Serves 4**

8 slices whole grain bread
6 tablespoons almond butter
2 bananas, peeled and thinly sliced

1½ tablespoons honey
Ground cinnamon, for sprinkling

Spread one side of each bread slice with the almond butter. Top each of 4 bread slices with the banana slices. Drizzle the remaining bread slices with the honey and sprinkle with cinnamon. Sandwich the bread slices together and serve.

Tip

Avoid the Burn

Don't forget the sunscreen—especially when you're picnicking with the kids! No matter if you're four or forty-four, nothing is worse than a day-after-picnic burn.

TGIF Chicken Salad Wraps with Pimiento

Back when Mama first started her empire with The Bag Lady sandwiches, she always made something special for her customers to look forward to for Friday lunches. And wouldn't you know, the hands-down most popular Friday lunch was chicken salad! This is our wrapped version of her TGIF favorite. **Serves 4**

5 cups chopped cooked chicken	**2 tablespoons whole grain mustard**
½ cup sliced pimientos	**1 tablespoon plus 1 teaspoon apple cider vinegar**
6 tablespoons chopped celery	**Salt and freshly ground black pepper**
6 tablespoons mayonnaise	**Four 9½-inch jumbo whole wheat honey tortilla wraps**
¼ cup chopped scallions (white and light green parts)	**1 cup loosely packed baby spinach leaves**

1. In a large bowl, combine the chicken, pimientos, celery, mayonnaise, scallions, mustard, vinegar, salt, and pepper.

2. Spoon one-quarter of the chicken salad onto each tortilla, leaving a ½-inch border around the edges, and top each tortilla with ¼ cup spinach leaves. Fold in one side of the wrap and roll up. Wrap tightly with aluminum foil (this helps to keep its shape) to transport. Remove the foil to serve.

Turkey and Pepper Jack Sammies with Chunky Avocado Salsa

We call for toasting the bread in the skillet. It's just a little touch that makes this sandwich, which is almost like a melt, extra crispy and extra tasty when you pull it out of the picnic basket. This sandwich is also great served hot—so bring it straight out to the back deck or patio as well as to the park. **Serves 4**

1 ripe avocado, halved, peeled, pitted, and diced	**¼ teaspoon salt**
2 tablespoons mayonnaise	**8 slices whole grain bread**
1 tablespoon chopped fresh cilantro	**¼ pound sliced deli smoked turkey breast**
2 teaspoons finely chopped red onion	**4 ounces pepper Jack cheese, thinly sliced**
2 teaspoons freshly squeezed lime juice	**Olive oil, for brushing**
½ jalapeño pepper, seeded and finely chopped	

1. In a medium bowl, mash together the avocado, mayonnaise, cilantro, onion, lime juice, jalapeño, and salt until almost smooth, but still slightly chunky.

2. Spread one side of each bread slice with the avocado salsa. Top each of 4 slices with the turkey and pepper Jack cheese, cover with the remaining slices, and serve.

3. Heat a large skillet over medium heat. Brush the tops and bottoms of the sandwiches with olive oil. Toast the sandwiches until the bread is crisp and golden and the cheese is melted, about 2 minutes per side. Serve hot or at room temperature.

Tuna Salad Wheels

Using spinach tortillas instead of bread makes for a wrap-style sandwich that's as pleasing to the eye as it is satisfying to carb counters. When assembling them for transport, secure the wheels with toothpicks and you'll be good to go. **Serves 4 to 6**

Four 5-ounce cans tuna packed in water, drained
¾ cup grated carrots
6 tablespoons mayonnaise
¼ cup pitted kalamata olives, chopped
¼ cup minced red onion

½ teaspoon kosher salt
½ teaspoon freshly ground black pepper
Four 8-inch spinach tortillas
Shredded iceberg or Boston lettuce

1. In a large bowl, combine the tuna, carrots, mayonnaise, olives, onion, salt, and pepper.

2. Spread one-quarter of the filling over each tortilla. Top with the lettuce. Roll up the tortillas over the filling and cut each crosswise on the diagonal into 1-inch-thick pinwheels.

8
Salads That Travel

Mediterranean Orzo Salad with Olives, Sun-Dried Tomatoes, and Pine Nuts

This is what Jamie and Brooke always bring on date night in Savannah's historic Forsyth Park to hear the symphony play. It's an elegant little salad that travels well, and there's no garlic in the dressing—just perfect for a romantic evening under the stars. **Serves 4**

1 cup orzo	**¼ teaspoon kosher salt, plus additional to taste**
3 tablespoons olive oil	**¼ teaspoon freshly ground black pepper**
½ teaspoon finely grated orange zest	**¼ cup pitted, sliced kalamata olives**
2 tablespoons freshly squeezed orange juice	**2 tablespoons coarsely chopped sun-dried tomatoes**
1½ teaspoons freshly squeezed lemon juice	**3 tablespoons toasted pine nuts**
2 tablespoons chopped fresh basil	

1. Cook the orzo according to the package directions. Drain and let cool. (You should have about 3 cups cooked orzo.)

2. In a small bowl, whisk together the olive oil, orange zest, orange juice, lemon juice, basil, ¼ teaspoon salt, and the pepper.

3. Transfer the orzo to a large bowl. Stir in the olives, sun-dried tomatoes, and pine nuts. Pour in the citrus dressing and toss to combine. Taste and adjust the seasoning, if necessary.

Keep a Lid on It

Transport pasta salads or other sides to the picnic in large lidded mason jars. You can buy the jars at most hardware stores—save the shallow box they come in to carry the jars to the picnic. Old-fashioned jars help to keep the bugs away, the salads fresh, and cut down on waste. Plus, they're just pretty!

Peppery Tuna Macaroni Salad

This starts off like many a tasty tuna salad, but then the hot pepper flavor sneaks up to really dazzle. You can find hot pickled peppers in the Latin food section of many supermarkets, but if you can't get them, just substitute a few dashes of Tabasco for a similar kick. The longer this side-dish salad sits in the fridge or cooler, the spicier it gets. **Serves 6 to 8**

1½ cups elbow macaroni

3 tablespoons mayonnaise

3 tablespoons sour cream

2 teaspoons white wine vinegar

1 small hot pickled pepper, such as peperoncini, minced

2 to 3 dashes hot pickled pepper pickling brine, or to taste

½ teaspoon freshly ground black pepper

Salt

One 10-ounce can white tuna packed in water, drained

½ cup grated carrots

2 tablespoons chopped fresh chives

1. Cook the macaroni according to the package directions. Drain, rinse with cold water, and drain again.

2. Meanwhile, in a medium bowl, whisk together the mayonnaise, sour cream, vinegar, pickled pepper, pepper brine, black pepper, and salt. Add the macaroni, tuna, carrots, and chives and toss to combine. Taste and adjust the seasoning, if necessary.

Classic Southern Slaw

We always had a batch of slaw in our fridge when we were growing up. Sometimes we ate it just on its own, but more often than not it was gobbled up as a condiment for sandwiches. Use it anytime you might normally slather on the mayonnaise—the slaw has mayo in it, so you'll still be getting the creamy element, but you'll get the added benefit of crunchy vegetables and less fat. Good thing it's so easy to make. You may find you need to replenish your slaw supply every other day. You can find prepared slaw mix in the vegetable section of your supermarket—takes all the work out of making this Southern favorite. **Serves 6**

½ cup mayonnaise
3 tablespoons finely chopped red onion
1½ tablespoons apple cider vinegar
1 teaspoon celery seed

½ teaspoon kosher salt
½ teaspoon freshly ground black pepper
¼ teaspoon Tabasco or other hot sauce
One 14- to 16-ounce package prepared slaw mix

1. In a small bowl, combine the mayonnaise, onion, vinegar, celery seed, salt, pepper, and Tabasco.

2. Place the slaw mix in a large bowl. Pour the mayonnaise mixture over the slaw and toss well. Let stand for 15 minutes before serving. The slaw will keep in an airtight container in the refrigerator for up to 5 days.

Lemon-Basil Green Bean Almondine Salad

This is our riff on the classic green bean almondine. We think it's at its most delicious with a light lemon-basil dressing. Be sure not to overcook the beans—they should make a real crunch when you dig in! **Serves 6**

1 pound fresh green beans, trimmed	**2 tablespoons chopped fresh basil**
½ cup slivered almonds	**1 large garlic clove, finely chopped**
3 tablespoons olive oil	**½ teaspoon salt**
2 tablespoons freshly squeezed lemon juice	**½ teaspoon freshly ground black pepper**

1. Bring a large pot of salted water to a boil. Have ready a bowl of ice water.

2. Drop the beans into the boiling water and cook until crisp-tender, 1 to 2 minutes. Use a slotted spoon to remove the beans. Transfer them immediately to the ice water to stop the cooking. Drain well and place the beans in a large bowl.

3. Toast the almonds in a small skillet over medium-high heat until golden, 2 to 3 minutes.

4. In a small bowl, whisk together the olive oil, lemon juice, basil, garlic, salt, and pepper.

5. Pour the lemon-basil dressing over the beans and toss well to combine. Sprinkle the almonds over the top of the salad and serve.

Layered Mandarin Orange Salad

The oranges add a light and juicy element to this pretty picnic dish. We find that a little touch of sweetness makes kids more likely to eat their salad. **Serves 4 to 6**

4½ cups shredded iceberg lettuce
One 15-ounce can mandarin orange segments, drained

½ cup slivered almonds, toasted if desired
½ cup prepared poppy seed dressing

In a medium bowl (with a lid, if taking the salad on the road), layer half the lettuce, half the orange segments, half the almonds, and half the poppy seed dressing. Repeat the layers, ending with the dressing. Chill in the refrigerator or a cooler until ready to serve or up to 4 hours.

Sweet Salads Tempt Young Eaters

Layered salads are not only a great way to clean out the fridge (because they use a small amount of a lot of ingredients), they're also a great way to get kids to eat their greens. Adding slightly sweet treats like mandarin oranges will tempt even picky eaters to clean their plates.

Broccoli Salad with Walnuts and Raisins

Broccoli is one of those powerhouse vegetables—its health benefits just boggle the mind. It's packed with folic acid, vitamin C, and more calcium than most dairy products. You wouldn't know how healthy you're eating from the taste of it. We can't get enough of this salad with its crunchy-sweet-savory combo of walnuts, raisins, and scallions. **Serves 6**

½ cup coarsely chopped walnuts
One 1-pound head broccoli, cut into ½-inch florets
½ cup mayonnaise
1 tablespoon balsamic vinegar
½ teaspoon salt

¼ teaspoon freshly ground black pepper
½ cup golden raisins
¼ cup chopped scallions (white and light green parts)

1. Preheat the oven to 350°F.

2. Spread the walnuts in a single layer on a baking sheet. Bake until fragrant and golden, about 5 minutes.

3. Bring a large pot of salted water to a boil. Have ready a bowl of ice water.

4. Drop the broccoli into the boiling water and cook until crisp-tender, 1 to 2 minutes. Use a slotted spoon to remove the broccoli. Transfer it immediately to the ice water to stop the cooking. Drain well and place the broccoli in a large bowl.

5. In a small bowl, whisk together the mayonnaise, vinegar, salt, and pepper. Spoon over the broccoli and stir to combine. Stir in the walnuts, raisins, and scallions and serve.

Muffuletta Salad

Another salad that got its inspiration from NOLA's French Quarter. Basically, it's our take on Central Grocery's famous sandwich, only served in a salad bowl, and it's a meal unto itself. This salad is fantastic for picnics as it really travels well, though if you prefer your croutons to have a little crunch, pack them in a resealable plastic bag, and toss them in right before serving. These days, you can find specialty lunch meats like mortadella and Genoa salami, as well as peperoncini, in the deli aisle of your supermarket, and bocconcini (mini balls of high-quality mozzarella) packed in oil at the deli counter. **Serves 8**

For the croutons

¼ pound day-old Italian bread, cut into 1-inch cubes
2 tablespoons olive oil
Large pinch of salt

For the dressing

3 tablespoons red wine vinegar
2 tablespoons minced hot pickled peppers, such as peperoncini
2 small garlic cloves, minced
½ teaspoon salt
½ teaspoon freshly ground black pepper
6 tablespoons olive oil
¼ cup pitted, sliced kalamata olives
¼ cup sliced pimiento-stuffed olives

For the salad

2 heads romaine lettuce, cored and chopped
½ pound bocconcini, halved, or cubed fresh mozzarella cheese (1⅓ cups)
¼ pound thinly sliced mortadella, cut into 1-inch pieces (1 cup)
¼ pound thinly sliced deli ham, cut into 1-inch pieces (1 cup)
¼ pound thinly sliced Genoa salami, cut into 1-inch pieces (1 cup)
3 ounces sliced provolone cheese, cut into 1-inch pieces (⅔ cup)

1. To make the croutons, preheat the oven to 300°F. Toss the bread cubes with the olive oil and salt. Spread the bread cubes in a single layer on a large baking sheet. Toast, tossing occasionally, until golden, about 15 minutes.

2. To make the dressing, in a medium bowl, whisk together the vinegar, pickled peppers, garlic, salt, and black pepper. Whisk in the olive oil, kalamata olives, and pimiento olives.

3. To make the salad, in a large salad bowl, toss the romaine with the bocconcini, mortadella, ham, salami, provolone cheese, and croutons. Pour the dressing over the salad and toss to combine well. Serve immediately.

NOLA-Style Dirty Rice Salad

We love New Orleans and try to get there every chance we get to have some of that delicious NOLA cooking. Dirty rice, a traditional Cajun dish usually made with crumbled sausage, bell peppers, onions, and celery, is one of Jamie's favorites to make at home when he wants a taste of the Crescent City. It was natural that one day the leftovers would find their way into a salad. **Serves 8**

1½ cups long-grain white rice	⅓ cup diced green bell pepper
¼ cup olive oil	¼ cup diced celery
½ pound Italian sausages, casings removed	¼ cup diced Vidalia onion
1½ tablespoons red wine vinegar	2 teaspoons minced jalapeño pepper
½ cup chopped fresh parsley or cilantro	½ teaspoon kosher salt, plus additional to taste
⅓ cup diced red bell pepper	½ teaspoon Tabasco or other hot sauce

1. Bring the rice and 2¾ cups water to a boil in a medium pot. Reduce the heat to a simmer, cover, and cook until tender and most of the liquid has evaporated, 17 to 20 minutes. Remove from the heat and let stand, covered, for 5 minutes. Fluff with a fork and transfer the rice to a large bowl.

2. Heat 1 tablespoon of the olive oil in a medium skillet over medium-high heat. Crumble in the sausage and cook until well browned, about 5 minutes. Remove from the heat and immediately stir in the vinegar, scraping up any browned bits from the bottom of the skillet.

3. Scrape the sausage and pan drippings into the bowl of rice. Add the remaining 3 tablespoons olive oil, the parsley, red bell pepper, green bell pepper, celery, onion, jalapeño, salt, and Tabasco; toss well. Taste and adjust the seasonings, if necessary.

Crumbled Corn Bread Salad with Black Beans, Red Bell Peppers, and Cherry Tomatoes

Here's another solution for using up leftover corn bread. In fact, this salad seems to work even better with corn bread that is one or two days old. If you're taking a long drive to your picnic, pack the corn bread separately and toss it in right before serving. **Serves 6 to 8**

6 ounces corn bread, roughly crumbled (about 1½ cups)	**1 cup canned black beans, rinsed and drained**
3 tablespoons olive oil	**¾ cup diced red bell peppers**
4 teaspoons red wine vinegar	**½ cup cherry tomatoes, quartered**
½ teaspoon salt	**¼ cup thinly sliced scallions (white and light green parts)**
½ teaspoon freshly ground black pepper	**2 tablespoons chopped fresh basil**

1. Place an oven rack 6 inches from the heat source and preheat the broiler.

2. Place the corn bread on a baking sheet and toast under the broiler until golden and crisp, about 3 minutes (check often to see that the crumbs do not burn). Transfer to a large salad bowl.

3. In a small bowl, whisk together the olive oil, vinegar, salt, and pepper.

4. Add the black beans, bell peppers, tomatoes, scallions, and basil to the salad bowl and toss gently. Pour the vinaigrette over the salad and toss to combine well. Serve immediately.

A Little Something Sweet GRILLED BANANA SPLITS

When we were kids, there was no better, more hoped for dessert than a banana split. And now that we're all grown up, one made with buttery grilled bananas is the perfect dessert for any age! **Serves 4**

4 large bananas
4 tablespoons butter, melted
1 pint of your favorite ice cream
Chocolate sauce, for serving
Chopped toasted nuts, for serving
Maraschino cherries, for serving

1. Preheat the grill to medium heat.

2. Brush the bananas with the melted buttter and place them on the grill. Grill, turning once, just until the bananas brown, about 3 minutes.

3. Split each banana and place both halves in a dish. Place scoops of your favorite ice cream in between the halves, add a drizzle of chocolate sauce and a sprinkle of chopped nuts—and don't forget the cherry on top!

9

Finger Foods, Dips, and Nibbles

Pickled Shrimp and Vidalia Onions

Pickled shrimp is a favorite of Mama's, and just about anyone who grew up in the South is right there with her. Mama adds hard-boiled eggs to her pickled shrimp jar, but we always do ours with Vidalia onions. Make sure you allow yourself enough pickling time—it takes twenty-four hours to make a nice jar of pickled shrimp. It's such a pretty sight—it works as a snack and also as a centerpiece for the picnic blanket.

Makes 1 quart pickled shrimp; serves 6

½ cup distilled white vinegar

2 tablespoons pickling spice

1 tablespoon sugar

2 garlic cloves, peeled and smashed

½ teaspoon salt

1 pound large shrimp, peeled and deveined

½ Vidalia onion, thinly sliced

1. In a medium saucepan over medium-high heat, combine the vinegar, 1 cup water, the pickling spice, sugar, garlic, and salt. Bring to a boil. Add the shrimp and onion and immediately reduce the heat to a simmer. Cook until the shrimp are just opaque, about 3 minutes.

2. Pour the hot mixture into a large, clean canning jar. Let cool, uncovered. Place the lid on the jar and close tightly. Refrigerate for at least 24 hours before serving.

Red Deviled Eggs

Deviled eggs are a classic and a must-have for any of our family get-togethers—probably lots of other families in America feel the same. Sometimes it's nice to add a twist to an old favorite; that's why we came up with these fun snacks. They're extra colorful to compete with the beauty of the great outdoors. To keep them looking their best, transport the egg halves separately from the filling. Store the filling in a pastry bag or a resealable plastic bag and when you're ready to serve, pipe the filling into the eggs.

Makes 24 deviled eggs

12 large eggs	2¼ teaspoons apple cider vinegar
6 tablespoons minced pimiento	¾ teaspoon salt
3 tablespoons ketchup	¾ teaspoon freshly ground black pepper
3 tablespoons mayonnaise	Sweet paprika, for serving

1. Place the eggs in a medium pot and cover with cold water. Bring to a boil over high heat. Immediately remove the pot from the heat, cover it, and let stand for 10 minutes. Uncover the pot and let the eggs cool in the water.

2. Once the eggs have cooled, peel them and halve them lengthwise. Carefully pop out the yolks and drop them into a medium bowl. Arrange the egg whites in a single layer on a large platter if filling immediately, or transfer, stacked, to a sturdy, airtight container for transport.

3. Mash the egg yolks lightly with a fork. Stir in the pimiento, ketchup, mayonnaise, vinegar, salt, and pepper. Place the filling in a pastry bag or a resealable plastic bag with one corner end snipped off (if you are traveling with the eggs, wait until you are ready to fill them before snipping the bag).

4. Pipe some filling into each egg white cavity. Sprinkle the tops of the eggs with paprika and serve.

Picnic Away Rainy Day Blues

Cooped up with the kids on a rainy day? Spread out a blanket on the living room floor for an indoor picnic. Sometimes just a lunchtime change of venue, moving from the table to the floor, makes the kind of family memories that last a lifetime.

Georgia Caviar

Did you think caviar meant fish eggs? Not in Georgia it doesn't! This dip has been one of Mama's favorite recipes since we can't remember when, and you'll find that it makes appearances on The Lady & Sons' buffet table. The flavors get better and better as it sits, which makes it a favorite to bring along on a picnic. We like to snack on it while sipping (what else?) Georgia Peach Punch (page 199). **Serves 6 to 8**

Two 15-ounce cans black-eyed peas, rinsed and drained	**3 jalapeño peppers, seeded and minced**
2 cups diced red bell peppers	**One 4-ounce jar diced pimiento**
⅔ cup diced tomatoes	**⅔ cup prepared Italian dressing**
½ cup diced onion	**Chopped fresh parsley, for garnish**
	Corn chips, for dipping

In a large bowl, combine the black-eyed peas, bell peppers, tomatoes, onion, jalapeños, and pimiento. Stir in the Italian dressing. Sprinkle with parsley and serve with corn chips for dipping.

Making Meals, One Nibble at a Time

Picnics can be such a fun social time with family and friends that sometimes we like to make a whole meal out of finger foods and nibbles. Serving Georgia Caviar (see above), Mini Potato Chip Frittatas (page 165), Red Deviled Eggs (page 163), and the like lets people stop by the blanket to graze and chat—then run back to the grass for three-legged races, horseshoes, touch football, and other outdoor activities.

Mini Potato Chip Frittatas

A full meal in a snack-size portion. These little potato chip ham-and-eggs hybrids are the product of a little late-night kitchen creativity that has found its way into our picnic basket and become a family favorite. Mama and Uncle Bubba just adore them. Serve 'em hot or at room temperature; either way they're fantastic!

Makes 12 frittatas; serves 6

10 large eggs
½ teaspoon salt
½ teaspoon freshly ground black pepper
¼ teaspoon sweet paprika

1½ cups lightly crushed potato chips
¼ pound thinly sliced deli ham, diced
2 tablespoons finely chopped scallions

1. Preheat the oven to 325°F. Spray a 12-cup muffin pan lightly with nonstick cooking spray.

2. In a large bowl, whisk together the eggs, salt, pepper, and paprika. Stir in the crushed potato chips, ham, and scallions.

3. Divide the mixture among the muffin cups, filling each three-quarters full.

4. Bake until the frittatas are cooked through, 12 to 15 minutes. Run a knife around the edges to loosen them. Pop out the frittatas and serve.

Home-Baked Tortilla Chips with Two Kinds of Salsa (Green Tomato and Fresh Pineapple)

Whether we're eating them at the stadium, in the park, or in front of the TV, our family and friends can go through a bag of tortilla chips and a jar of salsa in a matter of minutes. Not only is it more economical to make your snacking staples at home, it is loads more tasty—and lower in fat because the chips are baked rather than fried. Tortilla chips made from strips of corn tortillas just can't be beat, and these two salsa recipes are so wonderful in their own special ways that we just had to include them both. The green tomato salsa is a spicy dip—fresh tasting with more than a little heat—and the fresh pineapple salsa is perfect for snackers who like a bit of sweetness on their chips. These chips go great with a lighter, brighter sipper, such as our Cucumber Sangría (page 197). **Serves 6 to 8**

For the tortilla chips

Two 7.5-ounce packages 5½-inch corn tortillas (12 tortillas)
¼ cup olive oil
1½ teaspoons salt

For the green tomato salsa

¾ pound green tomatoes, cored and cut into wedges
3 scallions, trimmed
2 garlic cloves, unpeeled
1 tablespoon olive oil
½ cup chopped fresh cilantro
1 tablespoon freshly squeezed lime juice
½ teaspoon salt
¼ teaspoon Tabasco or other hot sauce, or to taste

For the pineapple salsa

1½ cups diced fresh pineapple
½ cup chopped cherry tomatoes
2 tablespoons chopped fresh cilantro
1½ tablespoons finely chopped red onion
1 jalapeño pepper, seeded and minced
2 teaspoons freshly squeezed lemon juice
½ teaspoon salt

1. To make the chips, preheat the oven to 350°F. Arrange the tortillas in a stack (do this in batches) and cut the stack into 6 equal triangles. In a bowl, toss the tortillas with the olive oil and salt.

2. Spread the tortillas in a single layer on two large baking sheets. Bake, tossing occasionally, until crisp and golden, 20 to 25 minutes. Let cool. (Makes about 4 cups.)

3. To make the green tomato salsa, increase the oven temperature to 375°F. In a large bowl, toss together the green tomatoes, scallions, garlic, and olive oil. Transfer to a baking sheet and roast until the veggies are caramelized and soft, about 30 minutes.

4. Squeeze the roasted garlic cloves from their peels, discarding the peels. Transfer the roasted vegetables to the bowl of a food processor. Add the cilantro, lime juice, salt, and Tabasco. Purée until smooth. Pour the salsa into a bowl and let cool. (Makes about 1¼ cups.)

5. To make the pineapple salsa, in a medium bowl, combine the pineapple, cherry tomatoes, cilantro, onion, jalapeño, lemon juice, and salt. (Makes about 1½ cups.)

6. Serve the salsas with chips for dipping.

Vidalia Onion and Beer Dip

This is the dip Uncle Bubba is famous for. Fresh herbs, Vidalia onion, and a little brew liven up onion soup mix like nobody's business. We wonder if this dip may not be the number-one reason Bubba gets so many invitations on Super Bowl Sunday. **Serves 8**

1½ tablespoons unsalted butter
1 medium Vidalia onion, thinly sliced
½ teaspoon dried thyme
¼ cup beer
One 8-ounce package cream cheese, softened

½ cup sour cream
1 tablespoon onion soup and dip mix
½ cup chopped fresh parsley
Potato chips or pretzels, for dipping

1. Melt the butter in a large skillet over medium-high heat. Add the onion and thyme and toss well. Cook, tossing occasionally, until the onion is tender and light golden, 10 to 15 minutes.

2. Stir in the beer and cook until the liquid has almost evaporated, about 2 minutes. Remove from the heat.

3. In a large bowl, fold together the cream cheese, sour cream, warm onion (this will help melt away any remaining cream cheese lumps), onion soup mix, and parsley.

4. Serve at room temperature or chill for 30 minutes and serve with potato chips or pretzels, for dipping.

Fresh Flavored Water

Whenever you're outdoors, especially when you've got the kids keeping you on your toes, you want to stay hydrated. Sometimes the young ones turn up their noses at a glass of plain water, but you may not want to add powdered fruit drink mix because of all that extra sugar. We like to add thinly sliced citrus fruits, berries, watermelon, or even cucumbers to our bottles of picnic water for a subtle and healthful flavoring.

Southern Snacking Bacon and Nuts

This sweet-salty-spicy snack gives everybody just the pick-me-up protein punch needed to keep the picnic fun going. Paula and Mike have been known to call time-outs on the Frisbee toss just to grab a handful. We make sure to have some on hand for every family party, whether it's indoors or outdoors.

Makes 2 cups nuts

2 cups unsalted roasted mixed nuts	½ teaspoon cayenne pepper
1 egg white, lightly beaten	⅛ teaspoon ground cinnamon
2 tablespoons granulated sugar	¾ pound sliced bacon
½ teaspoon salt	½ cup packed light brown sugar

1. Preheat the oven to 325°F.

2. In a bowl, toss the nuts with just enough egg white to coat. Stir in the granulated sugar, salt, cayenne, and cinnamon.

3. Spread out the nuts on a large baking sheet. Roast, stirring frequently, until the nuts are browned and almost dry to the touch, 12 to 15 minutes. Break up any clumps while the nuts are still warm. Transfer them to a medium bowl.

4. Increase the oven temperature to 350°F. Line a baking sheet with a nonstick liner or parchment paper sprayed with nonstick cooking spray.

5. Arrange the bacon in a single layer on the lined baking sheet. Sprinkle the bacon with a thin, even layer of brown sugar, coating both sides. Bake until crisp and golden, 20 to 25 minutes.

6. Transfer the bacon to a wire rack set over a rimmed baking sheet (or paper towels) to cool. Break the bacon into bite-size pieces and mix it into the nuts. Serve immediately or store in an airtight container for up to 2 days.

Southern Biscuit Cheese Straws

Mama has always told us to keep a can of ready-made biscuit dough in the house, in case we need to feed any hungry guests—and when your mama is Paula Deen, you know you'd best live by her advice, especially when it comes to matters of the stomach. These biscuit-dough cheese straws just explode with cheese flavor and are a breeze to put together whenever company comes a callin'. And when you serve these cheese straws with a Beer Can Shandy (page 197), you've got all the makings of a beautiful day. **Makes 8 twists**

One 16.3-ounce can jumbo refrigerated buttermilk biscuits (8 biscuits)

1 large egg, lightly beaten
1¼ cups grated Gruyère cheese (5 ounces)

1. Preheat the oven to 375°F. Grease a large baking sheet with butter or spray with nonstick cooking spray.

2. Cut each biscuit crosswise in half and roll the dough between your palms until each half forms a rope about 8 inches in length. Twist 2 ropes together, pressing the ends together to seal. Transfer the twists to the baking sheet.

3. Brush each twist with egg and sprinkle with the Gruyère cheese. Bake until golden, 12 to 15 minutes.

Chicken and Peanut Meatballs

Here are some flavorful little mouthfuls that would be just right to serve either at a fancy cocktail party or alongside the chips and dips at a family game night. Chopped peanuts are an unexpected pairing with ground chicken, but somehow it all comes together with a happy crunch. We use panko bread crumbs because they're just a little bit crispier and lighter than regular bread crumbs. You'll find them in the same aisle as the bread crumbs in the supermarket. **Makes about 2 dozen 1-inch balls**

¾ pound ground chicken
½ cup panko bread crumbs
¼ cup prepared peanut sauce, plus additional for dipping
3 tablespoons finely chopped salted roasted peanuts
3 tablespoons minced scallions (white and light green parts)

½ teaspoon salt, plus additional to taste
½ teaspoon Tabasco or other hot sauce
1 garlic clove, minced
Vegetable oil, for frying
Lime wedges, for serving

1. In a large bowl, mix together the chicken, panko, the ¼ cup peanut sauce, the peanuts, scallions, the ½ teaspoon salt, the Tabasco, and garlic until just combined. Roll the mixture into 1-inch balls and transfer to a large baking sheet.

2. Fill a large, deep skillet with 1 inch of vegetable oil. Heat the oil over medium-high heat until a drop of water sizzles in the pan.

3. Working in batches, fry the balls, turning frequently, until golden and cooked through, 2 to 3 minutes. Transfer to a paper-towel-lined plate and sprinkle lightly with the additional salt to taste. Serve with lime wedges and the additional peanut sauce.

Let the (Picnic) Games Begin!

While we adults might be happy to while away a summer afternoon simply by lounging on the picnic blanket, the kids will probably have other ideas of fun. Don't forget to bring the Frisbee and an assortment of balls to toss. And, for the bravest parents among us, we offer two words: *water balloons*.

On the Beach

This is the last section of the book, but in some ways, it's where the whole idea for *Get Fired Up* began: on the beach. Living right on the water here in Savannah, we boat over to Georgia's gorgeous coastal islands to spend days on the beach whenever we have the chance. We were kicking back on Little Tybee, an uninhabited island that you can camp on, and that you can see from Bobby's backyard, when the concept for this book came about.

We like to head over to Little Tybee with everything we need to make **The Deen Bros. Grilled Low Country Boil** (page 181), including some Old Bay, sausage, corn, and spuds. But on the day we started talking about doing another cookbook, we were making **Smoky Grilled Trout** (page 184) just like Mama always did when we vacationed in the Smoky Mountains as kids. The fresh-caught fish, the fresh air, and the sunset all combined to remind us of how much we love being outside, eating healthy food, and being together.

"We ought to do a book on fish and seafood," Bobby said. He was thinking about sharing some of our lighter recipes, like **Grilled Tuna Steak with Charred Corn Vinaigrette** (page 189). Of course, one thing led to another, as it will with us, and Jamie went from talking about doing his **Cedar Plank Salmon with Cucumbers and Sour Cream** (page 186) to figuring out a way to grill potato salad (we did it, see page 66). Before we knew it, we had decided to take on all of the Great Outdoors in this cookbook, from backyard to back of the car.

And it's with that beachy inspiration that we created our selection of cocktails and spiked punches. Each one is formulated to cool you down, just like a **Savannah Sea Breeze** (page 199) wafting through a Southern summer night. We also share our version of **Georgia Peach Punch** (page 199), with peach nectar to make it smooth and mellow and a little rum and amaretto for a kick. Lately, Bobby's taken to adding cucumber slices to his water after he comes back from a run, so we took that idea one step further and made **Cucumber Sangría** (page 197)—and nobody needs to work up a sweat in order to have a glass. As we like to say, "Life's a beach, man."

10

Dishes with Fishes

Fire-Roasted Clams and Mussels

This is the most affordable seafood dish around, with a flavor fit for a king. Clams and mussels done over the open flame are every bit as easy as on the stove top, but taste that much better when roasted outdoors. Make sure there's plenty of crusty bread to go around. Everyone's going to want it to sop up all the scrumptious juices. **Serves 4**

2 dozen littleneck or cherrystone clams, scrubbed and rinsed	**6 garlic cloves, thinly sliced**
2 pounds mussels, scrubbed and rinsed	**2 fresh rosemary sprigs**
⅓ cup olive oil	**½ teaspoon crushed red pepper flakes**
	Crusty bread, for serving

1. Place the clams and mussels in an aluminum roasting pan.

2. Heat the olive oil in a large skillet over medium heat. Add the garlic, rosemary, and red pepper flakes. Cook, stirring, until the mixture is fragrant, 1 to 2 minutes.

3. Pour the oil mixture over the clams and mussels and toss to combine.

4. Preheat the grill to medium heat.

5. Place the pan of clams and mussels on the grill. Close the cover and cook, stirring occasionally, until most of the clams and mussels have opened, 15 to 20 minutes.

6. Discard any unopened clams and mussels. Serve immediately, with bread for sopping up the juices.

The Deen Bros. Grilled Low Country Boil

Low Country boil, the classic spicy seafood and sausage dish of Southern coastal cooking, is a full meal that's a verified crowd-pleaser anytime you make it (and we make it every Friday night for The Lady & Sons' buffet). But if you're able to do it over the grill, it is truly spectacular. That smoky flavor will blow you away and, considering all you have to do is empty the grill basket onto newspaper atop a picnic table, it's certain this dish is made for outdoor enjoyment. **Serves 4**

¾ **pound small new potatoes**
1 large garlic clove, minced
Pinch of salt
6 tablespoons olive oil, plus additional for brushing
1½ tablespoons Old Bay seasoning
1 pound extra-large shrimp, shells intact

3 ears husked corn on the cob, cut crosswise in half
¾ **pound andouille sausage, cut crosswise into thirds**

Grill basket

1. Place the potatoes in a pot filled with salted water to cover. Bring to a boil over medium-high heat and boil until tender, 20 to 25 minutes. Drain well. Transfer the potatoes to a large bowl and cover with aluminum foil to keep them warm.

2. Meanwhile, use the flat side of a chef's knife to mash the garlic with the salt to form a paste. Transfer the garlic paste to a small bowl and whisk in the olive oil and Old Bay.

3. Place the shrimp in a bowl and pour in one-quarter of the oil mixture. Toss to coat. Brush the remaining oil mixture over the corn.

4. Preheat the grill to high and brush the grate with oil or spray with nonstick cooking spray.

5. Arrange the shrimp in a single layer in a grill basket. Transfer the basket to the grill. Place the corn and sausage on the grill next to the basket. Close the cover and cook, flipping the shrimp halfway through and turning the sausage and corn occasionally, until the shrimp are just opaque and the corn and sausage are golden, about 3 minutes per side.

6. Add the shrimp, corn, and sausage to the bowl of potatoes and toss well. Turn the food out onto a few sheets of newspaper and have at it.

Clean Up Clammy Hands

Paper napkins may not be enough for this low country boil. Squeeze fresh lemon juice on damp cloth towels to clean buttery, clammy fingers.

Grilled Lobster Tails with Spicy Butter

Anytime you serve lobster tails, you know it's a party in itself. Do the tails up right with our spicy butter sauce to make any occasion, even if it's simply celebrating a sunset with your sweetheart by your side, extra memorable. **Serves 4**

Four 8-ounce lobster tails
8 tablespoons (1 stick) unsalted butter
½ teaspoon salt

½ teaspoon cayenne pepper
¼ teaspoon freshly ground black pepper
Lemon wedges, for serving

---

1. Using kitchen shears, butterfly the lobster tails straight down the middle of the softer underside of the shells, snipping the meat down the center without cutting all the way through the bottom part of the shells.

2. In a small saucepan over medium heat, melt the butter, salt, cayenne, and black pepper.

3. Preheat the grill to medium-high heat and brush the grate with oil or spray with nonstick cooking spray.

4. Brush the lobster meat generously with the butter mixture, reserving some for serving. Transfer the lobster tails, cut side down, to the grill. Close the cover and cook, turning and basting occasionally, until the shells are bright red and the lobster meat is an opaque white, 8 to 10 minutes.

5. Remove the lobster tails from the grill and serve with the reserved butter mixture and the lemon wedges.

Outer Banks Crab Boil

April through October is prime season for blue crabs, and as good Southern boys, we feel obligated to eat our fill during those months! Fortunately for us, our Uncle Bubba is a champ with the crab net and always shows up around dinnertime with a whole slew of tasty crabs for us to cook up. This recipe couldn't be simpler, but that's how we like it here in the South—no frills to get in the way of our tasty catch.   **Serves 6**

¼ cup **Homemade Crab Boil Seasoning**
    (see below) or Old Bay seasoning
¼ cup **salt**
2 tablespoons **distilled white vinegar**

24 **live blue crabs**
Drawn butter, for serving
Crusty bread, for serving

1. Place a large pot of water on the grill and bring to a boil. Have ready a bucket of ice.

2. Add the Old Bay, salt, and vinegar to the pot and drop in half the crabs. Cover the pot and simmer for 15 minutes.

3. Remove the crabs with tongs and place in the bucket of ice to halt the cooking. Repeat with the remaining crabs.

4. Place the crabs on a newspaper-lined picnic table and serve with drawn butter, crusty bread, and plenty of napkins.

Homemade Crab Boil Seasoning

Makes about ¼ cup seasoning

1 tablespoon **celery seed**
1 tablespoon **whole black peppercorns**
6 **bay leaves**
4 **whole cloves**
1 teaspoon **sweet paprika**
½ teaspoon **whole cardamom**
½ teaspoon **mustard seed**
¼ teaspoon **ground mace**

In a clean coffee or spice grinder, grind all of the spices together. Store in an airtight container for up to 6 months.

Tip

Running Out of Ice Is Cold

Always bring two buckets of ice on boat trips—one bucket to dump on the crabs to keep them from overcooking and the other bucket for the beer (of course).

Smoky Grilled Trout

Isn't it crazy how certain tastes take you right back to days of your childhood? That's how it is for us when we make trout on the grill. One bite and it's like we are catapulted back to the trips we took with Mama and Daddy to go fishing and hiking in the Smoky Mountains. This is a little fancier presentation than Mama would do over our campfire; it's just a little improvement we've made over time. Of course, the best-tasting fish is the one you've caught yourself. **Serves 4**

Four ¾-pound whole butterflied trout (ask your fishmonger to do this for you)

Salt

1 teaspoon freshly ground black pepper, plus additional to taste

1 tablespoon olive oil

8 tablespoons (1 stick) unsalted butter

2 tablespoons chopped fresh thyme

2 teaspoons finely grated lemon zest

Grill basket

1. Use pliers or tweezers to remove any small pin bones from the fish cavities. Season the cavities lightly with salt and the additional pepper to taste. Rub the trout all over with the olive oil.

2. In a small saucepan, melt together the butter, thyme, lemon zest, and the 1 teaspoon pepper.

3. Preheat the grill to high heat.

4. Working in batches if necessary, place the trout in a grill basket. Transfer the basket to the grill. Close the cover and cook, turning the trout once halfway through, until the flesh is just opaque and flakes when prodded with a fork, 2 to 3 minutes per side.

5. Immediately brush the trout inside and out with the melted butter mixture and serve.

Glazed Barbecue Shrimp

Here in Savannah, we make shrimp every which way you can think of—including on the grill. This is the barbecue glaze we like to use whether we're making them for ourselves or for our guests at The Lady & Sons, where barbecue shrimp is always on the menu. We think this glaze is just a little more delicately flavored than our other barbecue sauce and brings out all the natural goodness of seafood. We could eat this all day long!

Serves 4 to 6

1½ pounds jumbo shrimp, peeled and deveined
½ teaspoon salt
¾ teaspoon freshly ground black pepper
⅔ cup homemade barbecue sauce (see page 10) or
   prepared barbecue sauce

⅓ cup apricot jam
2 teaspoons apple cider vinegar
¼ teaspoon crushed red pepper flakes

6 metal skewers

---

1. Rinse the shrimp and pat dry with paper towels. Season all over with the salt and pepper.

2. In a small bowl, whisk together the barbecue sauce, apricot jam, vinegar, and red pepper flakes. Toss two-thirds of the sauce with the shrimp; reserve the remaining one-third for basting.

3. Thread the shrimp through the head end and tail end and onto the skewers.

4. Preheat the grill to medium-high heat and brush the grate with oil or spray with nonstick cooking spray.

5. Transfer the skewers to the grill. Close the cover and cook for 1 minute per side. Baste the shrimp with the reserved sauce, close the cover, and cook for 30 seconds per side, or until the shrimp are opaque and well glazed.

Cedar Plank Salmon with Cucumbers and Sour Cream

Salmon is such a light and lovely fish. It has a real meaty texture, but it won't weigh you down like a thick piece of red meat might. Grilling fish over a cedar plank is a fun technique that adds a surprising amount of robust, smoky flavor without one single calorie—one of the reasons we like to add a little sour cream as a sauce, which will get sopped up nicely with a little Mediterranean Orzo Salad with Olives, Sun-Dried Tomatoes, and Pine Nuts (page 146), for example. **Serves 6**

1¼ teaspoons salt, plus additional to taste	3 small garlic cloves, minced
¾ cup sour cream	Six 8-ounce salmon fillets, skins on
6 tablespoons peeled, seeded, and diced cucumber	2 tablespoons olive oil
1½ tablespoons chopped fresh dill	Freshly ground black pepper
¾ teaspoon freshly squeezed lemon juice	Two 12 x 10-inch cedar planks, about ¾ inch thick

1. Soak the cedar planks in a large pan of water for 1 hour (see Note). Remove from the water and rub each plank with ½ teaspoon of the salt.

2. In a small bowl, whisk together the sour cream, cucumber, dill, lemon juice, garlic, and the remaining ¼ teaspoon salt. Taste and adjust the seasoning, if necessary. Cover with plastic wrap and refrigerate until ready to use or up to 4 hours.

3. Preheat the grill to high heat.

4. Brush the salmon with the olive oil and season with the additional salt and the pepper. Place 3 fillets, skin side down, on each plank. Transfer the planks to the grill. Close the cover, reduce the heat to medium-low, and cook until the surface fat on the salmon begins to turn white, 15 to 20 minutes.

5. Serve topped with a dollop of the cucumber and sour cream sauce.

Note: Cedar planks can be bought at cooking supply stores, such as Williams-Sonoma, but you can also get untreated cedar planks at many hardware and gardening supply stores. Simply submerge them in a sinkful of water for at least 1 hour or overnight before using them on the grill—they'll last longer the longer you soak them. It's time to get a new plank when the wood is scorched on both sides.

Grilled Tuna Steak with Charred Corn Vinaigrette

Tuna steaks are probably the easiest fish to grill. The preparation is similar to a beefsteak: Simply place over the heat and flip once. Make the tuna steak with this charred corn vinaigrette for an impressive meal that you can pull together in a matter of minutes. The vinaigrette also pairs well with grilled or roasted chicken.

Serves 4

For the vinaigrette

1 cup grilled corn kernels, cut from 1 cob
   (see Mexican Corn on the Cob, page 60)
¼ cup olive oil
2 tablespoons finely chopped fresh basil
2 teaspoons white wine vinegar
1 teaspoon finely chopped garlic
½ teaspoon salt
½ teaspoon freshly ground black pepper

For the tuna

2 teaspoons white wine vinegar
2 teaspoons honey
2 tablespoons olive oil
½ teaspoon salt
½ teaspoon freshly ground black pepper
Four 6- to 8-ounce yellowfin tuna steaks,
   rinsed and patted dry

1. To make the vinaigrette, in a small bowl, whisk together the corn, olive oil, basil, vinegar, garlic, salt, and pepper.

2. To make the tuna, in a wide, shallow bowl, whisk the vinegar with the honey until the honey dissolves. Whisk in the olive oil, salt, and pepper. Place the tuna steaks in the vinegar mixture and turn to coat.

3. Preheat the grill to medium-high heat and brush the grate with oil or spray with nonstick cooking spray.

4. Transfer the tuna steaks to the grill. Close the cover and cook to the desired doneness, 1½ to 2 minutes per side for medium-rare.

5. Serve the tuna with the corn vinaigrette spooned on top.

Blackened Catfish Po'boys with Grilled Tomatoes and Onions

Here's another dish we learned to make on our visits to New Orleans, our home away from home. You can't go a block without seeing a po'boy stand; po'boys are practically the Louisiana state sandwich. But you know what? They taste just as good in Georgia or in your home state, too! Here in the South, you can get catfish just about anywhere, but if you can't find any in your neck of the woods, then a mild-flavored fish such as tilapia makes a nice substitution. **Serves 6**

---

1 cup mayonnaise
¼ cup finely chopped pimiento
¼ cup finely chopped scallions (white and light green parts)
1 teaspoon Tabasco or other hot sauce
8 tablespoons (1 stick) unsalted butter, melted, plus additional for brushing

2 tablespoons Cajun spice mix
Six ⅓-pound skinless catfish or tilapia fillets, rinsed and patted dry
Six 8-inch hoagie rolls, split
3 cups shredded iceberg lettuce
2 medium tomatoes, thinly sliced

---

1. In a small bowl, whisk together the mayonnaise, pimiento, scallions, and Tabasco. Cover tightly with plastic wrap and refrigerate until ready to use.

2. In a wide, shallow bowl, whisk together the melted stick of butter and the Cajun spice mix. Dip the catfish fillets into the mixture.

3. Preheat the grill to high heat and brush the grate with oil or spray with nonstick cooking spray.

4. Transfer the catfish fillets to the grill. Close the cover and cook until the fillets flake easily with a fork, 2 to 3 minutes per side. Transfer the fillets to a plate.

5. Brush the cut sides of the rolls with the additional melted butter and place, cut side down, on the grill. Toast until lightly charred, 30 seconds to 1 minute.

6. Spread some of the mayonnaise mixture onto each toasted roll. Fill the sandwich with catfish, lettuce, and tomato slices and serve.

Grilled Crab Cake Sammies

Crab cakes done on the grill are every bit as tasty as when they're deep-fried, but a whole lot lighter on fat and calories. When you serve them as sandwiches, they're ideal for a day on the beach. Just put your crab cake sammie in one hand and catch the Frisbee in the other. **Serves 10**

1 pound crabmeat, picked over for shells or cartilage	1½ tablespoons **Dijon mustard**
¼ cup finely chopped **red bell pepper**	2 teaspoons **Old Bay seasoning**
1 **celery** stalk, finely chopped	½ teaspoon finely grated **lemon zest**
2 **scallions** (white and light green parts), finely chopped	½ teaspoon freshly ground **black pepper**
2 tablespoons **mayonnaise**	20 slices **white bread**, crusts removed
	Olive oil, for brushing

1. In a large bowl, fold together the crabmeat, bell pepper, celery, scallions, mayonnaise, mustard, Old Bay, lemon zest, and black pepper. Sandwich about ¼ cup crab mixture between 2 slices of the bread. Repeat with the remaining crab mixture and bread slices. Brush both sides of each sandwich with olive oil.

2. Preheat the grill to medium-high and brush the grate with oil or spray with nonstick cooking spray.

3. Transfer the sandwiches to the grill. Close the cover and cook, turning once, until both sides are golden and lightly charred, about 1 minute per side.

A Little Something Sweet **PIÑA COLADA FRUIT SKEWERS**

These dessert skewers get you in that tropical mood, and are a refreshing and fun way to end a meal outside. **Serves 6**

¾ pound peeled fresh pineapple, cut into 1-inch chunks
3 tablespoons light rum
1 tablespoon honey
Sweetened coconut flakes, for serving

6 metal skewers

1. Thread the pineapple chunks onto the skewers.
2. In a small bowl, mix together the rum and honey. Brush the pineapple generously with the rum mixture.
3. Preheat the grill to high heat and brush the grate with oil or spray with nonstick cooking spray.
4. Place the skewers on the grill. Close the cover and cook until the pineapple is light golden, 3 to 4 minutes per side. Sprinkle with the coconut before serving.

11

Seaside Sippers

Pomegranate Punch

We both got into drinking pomegranate juice because it's so healthy, and then we thought, why not add it to a punch? Here's hoping it cures the hangover before it starts! **Serves 8**

4 cups pomegranate juice	**Freshly squeezed juice of 2 limes**
2 cups seltzer	**Pomegranate seeds, for garnish (optional)**
1 cup vodka (optional)	**Lime wedges, for serving**

In a large pitcher or punch bowl, combine the pomegranate juice, seltzer, vodka (if using), and lime juice. Serve over ice, garnish with pomegranate seeds, if desired, and lime wedges.

Frosty Piña Colada Punch

We love the way the coconut sorbet keeps this punch cool without our having to water down the flavor with ice cubes—and it gives the taste of an island vacation right there in the punch bowl! **Serves 4**

2 cups pineapple juice	**2 cups seltzer**
1 cup light rum	**Pineapple slices, for garnish**
1 pint coconut sorbet	

In a large punch bowl, combine the pineapple juice and rum. Add the sorbet to the bowl in scoops. Just before serving, add the seltzer and garnish the bowl with pineapple slices.

Glassware and the Beach Don't Mix!

We like to feel the sand between our toes—not broken glass. Always use plastic cups (we're fond of the sturdy, reusable kind) to sip your seaside punch.

Cucumber Sangría

Usually sangría is made with just fruit, but we love to add sliced cucumber for a more mellow flavor.
Serves 6

One 750-milliliter bottle dry white wine	**1 English cucumber, rinsed and thinly sliced**
½ cup brandy	**1 green apple, cored, seeded, and thinly sliced**
1 cup green grapes, washed and halved	**1 cup seltzer**

In a large punch bowl or mason jar, combine the white wine, brandy, grapes, cucumber, and apple. Stir the mixture well, pressing the fruit to the bottom the bowl. Just before serving in cups with ice, add the seltzer.

Sparkling Strawberry Punch

When a punch tastes this good, you better believe all us guys will take a glass—even if it's pink! **Serves 6**

½ cup fresh or frozen strawberries, thawed (if using frozen)	**One 750-milliliter bottle sparkling wine, preferably rosé, chilled**
2 tablespoons sugar	

In a blender, purée the strawberries and sugar until smooth. Pour the purée into a large pitcher or punch bowl and add the sparkling wine, stirring just to combine.

Beer Can Shandies

This recipe comes courtesy of our Uncle Bubba, who is a genius when it comes to can-of-beer cuisine. This is a mouthwatering way to lighten up your lager when you're imbibing on a hot and sunny day. **Serves 6**

6 cans of your favorite lager	**One 16-ounce carton of your favorite lemonade**

Crack open your favorite beer. Take four sips. Top the remaining beer with your favorite lemonade. Swirl to combine, adding more lemonade as desired.

Washed Ashore (aka Tybee Island Cocktail)

This is just the perfect little beverage to sip when we're spending the day on Tybee Island. Coconut water (not to be confused with canned coconut milk) is very light and not too sweet. It really hits the spot after a day spent under the glare of a Georgia summer sun. **Serves 8**

4 cups coconut water, such as Zico	Crushed ice, for serving
2 cups dark rum	Lime wedges, for garnish

In a large pitcher, combine the coconut water and rum. Serve in glasses filled with crushed ice and garnished with a lime wedge.

Mug-a-Uga

This little cup of deliciousness is named in honor of Uga, the University of Georgia's trusty mascot (and a distant relative of Jamie's bulldog, Champ). Sip this on those nippy fall mornings when you're up early rooting for the home team. **Serves 4**

4 cups freshly brewed hot coffee	1 tablespoon plus 1 teaspoon dark brown sugar
½ cup Bourbon	Whipped cream, for serving
¼ cup Frangelico	

In a large thermos or carafe, combine the coffee, Bourbon, Frangelico, and brown sugar. Pour the drink into four mugs and top each with a dollop of whipped cream.

Georgia Peach Punch

This punch is as dreamy as a Savannah sunset right there in your glass—just the thing for an outdoor grilling party. **Serves 6**

One 32-ounce bottle peach nectar	**Freshly squeezed juice of 1 lime, or more to taste**
1 cup white rum	**Seltzer, to top off glasses**
½ cup amaretto	

In a large punch bowl, combine the peach nectar, rum, amaretto, and lime juice. Taste the punch and add more lime juice, if necessary. Serve with ice cubes, topping off each glass with seltzer.

Savannah Sea Breeze

We love to serve this punch every now and again to enjoy with the family on our porch. The blend of cranberry and grapefruit juice, topped with peach schnapps, gives just the right balance of tart and sweet to perk us up when we're all kicking back and watching the sun go down. **Serves 8**

8 cups cranberry juice	**Crushed ice, for serving**
2 cups vodka	**8 teaspoons peach schnapps**
2 cups grapefruit juice	**Fresh peach slices, for garnish**

In a large pitcher, combine the cranberry juice, vodka, and grapefruit juice. Pour into glasses filled with crushed ice and float 1 teaspoon peach schnapps on top. Garnish each glass with a fresh peach slice.

Acknowledgments

We would like to first thank and acknowledge our staff at The Lady & Sons restaurant for giving us the opportunity and ability to go outside of 102 West Congress Street. For many years we could never miss a day at the restaurant, and because of y'all, we are now able to grow our business in so many different ways. Thanks to Paula Deen Enterprises and Uncle Bubba's Oyster House for all the dedicated hard work and support as well.

Thank you to our talented editor, Pamela Cannon, for all of your efforts to help make this project a success, and to Libby McGuire and the entire Ballantine team for guiding us in the right direction and producing a beautiful book.

Thank you to Melissa Clark, again, for all of your recipe testing, late-night phone calls, flights to Savannah, and chasing the two of us around until we got it done. You deserve a medal.

Thank you to our team from New York, Janis Donnaud and Barry Weiner; without y'all, we could not have done it.

Thanks so much to Ben Fink for providing some of the most natural and beautiful photographs of the two of us at work and play. Somehow, Ben, you made us look good.

Thanks to Libbie Summers, our friend and the best damn food and set director anyone could wish for.

Thanks to Randy Davis of Davis Produce for supplying all those picture-perfect fruits and veggies and for letting us take photos at your Savannah produce stand.

Thank you to Ric Sisler and the Savannah Sand Gnats for allowing us onto the field at historic Grayson Stadium for some great photos.

All our love to Mom and Dad; without you, we really could not have done it.

And, as always, Jamie would like to say a special thank-you: To Brooke for my beautiful life and the gift of our son, Jack. Y'all make my world go around, and I love you both up to the sky.

Index

About the Authors

Jamie and **Bobby Deen** grew up in Georgia—first in Albany and then in Savannah—and, like many Southerners, they have always considered cooking and food a big part of their lives. When their mother, Paula Deen, started a sandwich delivery business in 1989, the boys took charge of deliveries. As the business grew into The Lady restaurant, they continued to help. Then, in 1996, the trio opened The Lady & Sons restaurant to resounding success. They haven't looked back since. They regularly appear on NBC's *Today* show and hosted their own Food Network show, *Road Tasted*.

Melissa Clark has written for *The New York Times, Food & Wine, Travel & Leisure,* and *Real Simple* and has authored or co-authored thirty books.